The Truth About
ANGELS

The Truth About

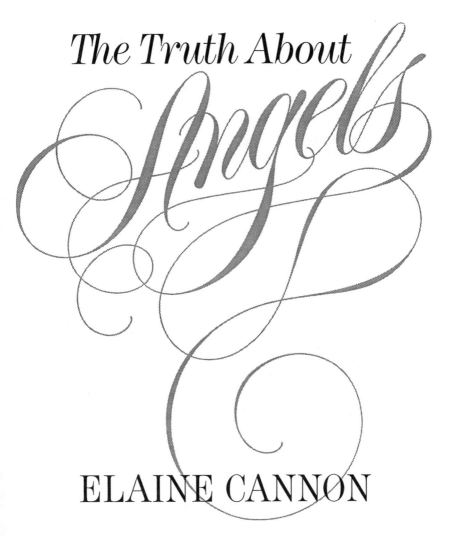

Angels

ELAINE CANNON

BOOKCRAFT
Salt Lake City, Utah

Library of Congress Catalog Card Number: 96–86546
ISBN 1–57008–289–8

Third Printing, 1997

Printed in the United States of America

Jesus "spake unto the multitude: . . .
Behold your little ones.
And as they looked to behold
they cast their eyes towards heaven,
and they saw the heavens open,
and they saw angels
descending out of heaven . . . ;
and the angels did minister unto them.
And the multitude did see and hear
and bear record;
and they know that their record is true
for they all of them did see and hear,
every man for himself;
and they were in number about
two thousand and five hundred souls;
and they did consist of men, women, and children."

3 Nephi 17:23–25

CONTENTS

CONTENTS

ACKNOWLEDGMENTS

I gratefully acknowledge that many have participated in producing *The Truth About Angels*. It takes more than the proverbial village and more than an afternoon for such a venture. The literature of our belief formed the basis for this book crafted by the skilled Bookcraft team. Centuries of wisdom to draw from has made the project fascinating. Reseeking details in beloved scriptures aroused new appreciation for early, inspired record keepers. Working with historians, librarians, docents, theologians, and conversant friends has been gratifying and enlightening. So that others might be lifted, many have graciously shared their sacred personal experiences. My debt to them is deep.

Joyful thanks to my stalwart daughters Carla, Susan, and Holly for being soul mates in the search for truth; to the inimitable LaVerkin Angel DeLoris Orvin, slave to wellness, for making it physically possible; and to Dan Hogan and Rebecca Taylor for their sensitive editing. Thanks also to Charles Jensen for a special perspective.

The gift of my own testimony certainly has cast its light on the fine points of sorting truth from error. Forever my gratitude belongs to God.

One

ANGELS AND
PEACEABLE THINGS

*G*od's angels are a thrilling study. Clearly, angels get around. They have mingled with the very elect in heaven and on earth. They have been on a first name basis with the prophets and patriarchs recorded in the stick of Judah and the stick of Joseph. They have dealt with kings and rulers of exotic lands and with anxiously engaged heroes and heroines of the Reformation and Restoration. But angels also have touched the humble among mortals. The scriptures affirm they have formed innumerable concourses between heaven and earth. Angels have been spectators to the world's vibrant moments and have participated in one way or another in the grandest—and the quietest—events along a course from the War in Heaven to the Garden of Eden; through the scattering of family tribes and covenant children; through the birth, trials, mission, crucifixion, and subsequent resurrection of

Christ; and on to the season of joy with the early Saints of the restoration of the fulness of the gospel!

And yet, when I set my foot to a path of searching out the truth about angels, I did so without the slightest idea of the vast amount of information on the subject of angels *nor the extent of theological error in religious collections!* It was alarming. The wide range of collections in Christian stores and the popularized and serious icons in secular boutiques attested to the perceived need and hope placed in manmade angel themes. The abundance of worldly data about angels is increasingly misleading, however well meaning. Henry David Thoreau's words lend some insight: "Many an object is not seen, though it falls within the range of our visual ray, because it does not come within the range of our intellectual ray." For example, a diseased tissue sample viewed through a microscope by a trained medical technician would reveal valuable information but would mean nothing to the eye of a plumber, a professional athlete, or a housewife.

In other words, if people do not understand God, they cannot know how to find the truth about the angels who serve him. Too many half-truths plague life today. Truth has been turned into error. For instance, the method of baptism has deteriorated from full immersion performed with God's authority to man-designed ceremonies of one kind or another. A satisfying symbol of cleansing and rebirth after the manner of Christ's own baptism and his commandments has been changed to a mere standing in a body of water or the convenient sprinkling on an infant's head. Some have written marriage ceremonies that have nothing to do with God and eternal commitment. Views on how angels look, where they live, what they do, and how they operate have changed vastly over the generations, which has led to a peculiar kind of idolatry by putting other gods before Him who is our Creator.

Every student of angelology can come to know the truth about angels. The Creator is our master teacher and the fulness of the revealed word of God is the text. He will help us learn, line upon line, all truth from which we can benefit.

What difference can it make to you to learn the truth about angels? For a beginning, you can have the same kind of *joyful awakening* that I have experienced in the years of preparing this book.

You will learn to *discern* fact from fantasy and eternal truth from shallow explanations of earth-tied thinkers.

You can develop *eyes that see* and a *heart that feels* the beautiful link between heaven's angels and earth's mortals; thus, you will better understand where we all fit into Heavenly Father's family.

You will be *comforted*. This is a sidebar to an acquaintance with angels. You see, this book is also for anyone who has lost a loved one or suffered the trauma of temptation.

You can be *fascinated by what angel study reveals* about temptations, life's challenges, human nature, individual life missions, and the awesome power of God.

You may happily be jogged into *giving credit where credit is due*. How blessed we are by Heavenly Father and the Lord Jesus Christ and the peaceable things of their kingdom! So much the better if learning the truth about angels both delights us and awakens us to God's sacred gift of angels in our midst, for, as Moroni said, "Neither have angels ceased to minister unto the children of men."[1]

Moroni should know.

Come, step into the world of God's wondrous creations. Feel yourself renewed, filled with awe at God's powers and creations—light and dark; dry branch and green bud; the diamond-studded heaven of a winter night; stretching sea and vastly varied land; every plant of the field, every yielding tree; herb, grass, and seed; the great whales, the winged owl, and every living creature that moves. God planned all this and *made it so,* including man and woman.

Angels, too.

NOTES

1. Moroni 7:29.

Two

ANGELS
IN OUR MIDST

$\mathcal{R}$esearch indicates that stories abound of people in our time who have had experiences with guardian angels, helpful heavenly hosts, and spirit messengers from God. Nearly all persons so blessed consider the experience sacred, personal, and rare. They have their own confirmation in heart and mind through the power of the Holy Ghost that indeed they have received a heaven-sent blessing, and no amount of public discussion or distortion, scoffing or doubt can change that.

People differ in their perspective of just what their supernatural experience was. Some consider Paul's counsel to the Hebrews as valid: "Be not forgetful to entertain strangers: for thereby some have entertained angels unawares."[1] Many openly acknowledge angels in our midst. Angels do still move among us, more widely than we may ever know because of the care that people give not to cast their pearls of celestial experience before the unappreciative.

To protect the privacy of the individuals involved in the accounts we include here, and to preserve the sacred nature of God's gift in sending his messengers, identity and some details may have been deliberately changed or withheld. But the edifying principles involved hold fast eternally.

*   *   *

A distinguished man lay in his bed dying. The struggle had been long and arduous. It was Daryl's turn to keep the night watch and relieve her mother, the man's exhausted wife. Daryl sat in a comfortable chair listening to the soft strains of classical music by which this sensitive, cultured man was comforted—hymns made him cry now.

Suddenly Daryl sensed an exhilarating *fulness* in the room. She became poignantly aware of wave after wave of people crowding the master bedroom where she kept a vigil by the beloved man's side! It was startling, incredible, reverently joyful—these angels were encircling his bed. She looked about but saw nothing different. Nevertheless not seeing did not change what she felt—crowded and tearful, she was a participant in a sacred spiritual experience. Daryl *knew* that the dying man's first wife was there (though she had never met this woman), and so was her own deceased father. Both of these people had passed forward to heaven about the same time a few years ago. She sensed the reality of men and women of all ages, and children as well. Daryl wondered, had these spirits gathered to usher this fine gentleman through the veil to heaven, into the same sociality they had enjoyed while they all were on earth?[2] It was humbling. Awesome.

Then Daryl heard anxious stirring in the bed, and she quickly inquired, "Are you all right?"

The answer was immediate and anxious: "I want to go home."

"Why don't you try to go to sleep?" Daryl tucked the covers about him. "There. It's all right. Rest."

And he did, taking his last earthly breath as angels ushered him home.

*   *   *

Rachel was a faithful, humble woman who was called to serve in a high position in the Church's auxiliaries. Details of her personal life made it extremely difficult for her to feel comfortable in accepting this new assignment. Some weeks before the call actually came, Rachel had received repeated messages on successive nights. She would be awakened by a voice warning her to get prepared for a specific Church appointment that was to come to her—and the appointment was stated. There also came to her clear instruction about certain things she was to do while in that position. After being set apart in her office of service, Rachel became conscious of a feeling that she described as "being ushered along, like a patient learning to walk again, followed by an aide with a wheelchair, or a toddler struggling with his first step beside a watchful mother."

She explained further: "I kept looking over my shoulder to see what was beside me. Sometimes I felt I could almost hear a rushing sound. I came to understand that I had a supporting host of angels about me—hovering, gently watchful, bearing me up. It was real! Looking back now at the way things fell into place, I know I was in the midst of angels. It was such a marvelous feeling that God was so mindful of me as I tried to do his work."

* * *

Johanna and Kent were caught on a freeway in a raging, blinding blizzard and ice storm. Kent later explained: "I am a stroke victim, so Johanna was doing the driving to a resort where I could rest up following hip surgery—on my good side, of course. I couldn't walk at all. So when a car in front of us braked suddenly, Johanna tried turning out to miss colliding; however, she lost control. Our car slid sideways off the road, over the shoulder, and into a deep ditch, where it came to rest against a barbed wire corral fence. Of course, immediately we prayed in gratitude and for help. We hadn't rolled over, but when Johanna got out of the car and surveyed the situation she could see immediately there was absolutely nothing we could do. She got back in and tried driving the car up and out. It only made matters worse. We knew that we were in trouble. Ice formed on the windshield. Visibility was zero. Traffic was heavy on the holiday weekend, and each driver had to watch out for his own path because the roads were deep drifts of snow over black ice. No one could see us down there or help us anyway. And I couldn't walk out! We were heading south to sun country, so we were ill-prepared for such a disaster. We had planned a gas stop at the next town, and so running our motor and heater for any length of time would be unwise and perhaps impossible."

Johanna told him later that when she had realized their plight and had gotten out of the car to tie her red scarf on the antenna, she cried out loud to Heavenly Father, "Please, please, please, dear Heavenly Father; please don't let my dear husband freeze to death here because I am an unskilled driver! Don't let him die in this helpless, frightening way."

Kent went on with the story: "Before her prayer was barely finished, a big government truck was able to stop above us on the shoulder. The driver slid over to the passenger side to exit the truck. He left the door open as he came down to survey our situation, but he explained that it was against government rules to pick up riders, even if we could figure a way to get a giant like me up the incline. He promised to go ahead to the next town and send help. Johanna, with sagging spirits, stood against the driver's door of our snow-bogged car and watched that government driver turn to hike up the impossible, slippery hill. Then a miracle! Just then a big old Buick sedan stopped right behind the government truck. A man in work overalls but no coat got out and walked easily down the slope, straight toward me, as if he already was aware of the details of my situation. He didn't say a word to anybody—just scooped me up in his arms like a baby and easily swept me up the incline and into the passenger's seat of the government vehicle! Without a word he was gone. Of course, government rules bowed to miraculous help—and help from a man whom we later learned was LDS.

Johanna cried all the way to the next town. We agreed it was our Three Nephites experience."

*   *   *

The following story is shared by Laura, who had a sister Elise, a young mother who had suffered greatly in her few years of marriage to an abusive husband who at last had been restrained by law to keep away from her. Through it all Elise had remained true and faithful as a leader of youth, until she finally failed fast to a mystery virus. When the following incident occurred, she lay near death in the hospital. Laura described the sacred experience:

"I had gone to visit Elise in the cardiac intensive care unit. She was very fragile and restless. However, she greeted me with her usual warmth and charm, calling me by name. She beckoned me close to her and whispered that there had been people surrounding her bed who wanted her, she said. 'There are people here—pushing me—they've come to get me to take me on a trip from which I will never return.' She confessed to me that she had argued with them, but when I came in they had gone away. Then she asked me to pray with her for peace from this feeling of darkness. The prayer was short, but we were blessed with a wonderful outpouring of the Spirit. I sat in a chair close to her bed, and we both dozed for a brief time. Suddenly I was startled by the sound of her voice. She was talking to someone else, absolutely oblivious of me.

"The spirit in the room was wonderfully enveloping. Elise was looking up toward the ceiling. Her face was radiant. It had changed—this attractive young mother who had been so ill now was extraordinarily beautiful, full of light and love. Her eyes were shining and her smile soft and sweet and wholesome as she talked earnestly to someone I couldn't see or hear. I could hear only her voice, but clearly she could see and hear her invisible-to-me visitor. Her conversation was appropriately paced, and from her response I perceived that she was needed in heaven and that her children on earth would be all right. She had struck a bargain with heaven for a little more time to get her family affairs in order.

"I stood there quietly watching until she closed her eyes and relaxed in the bed. I asked, 'Elise, honey, were you talking with the Lord?' She turned toward me and answered brightly, 'Almost!' Nothing more was ever said about this. She died in a couple of months, prepared to move on. As for myself, I felt gratitude for being allowed to witness such a lovely connection with heaven when Elise talked to her angel."

*   *   *

Angel stories confirm God's existence, prove God's power, underscore his love for us, and emphasize his mission to bring to pass the immortality and eternal life of everyone. It is for us to keep faithful so that we may be in a position to receive such unspeakable joy as he has in store for us.

*   *   *

David Wilson was the type and shadow of an unequivocally, all inclusive, loving and demonstrative young father. His life had been an incredible struggle since the day he was born. The day he died, David's many associates quietly celebrated his peace. For years David had looked forward to being on the same side of the veil as the Lord Jesus Christ. He wanted to be on the Lord's errand forever. However, no one had expected that angel duties—being a messenger from God to mortals—would begin so soon for David.

The night before David's funeral, a brother-in-law named Brent, who had lived a somewhat wayward life, was awakened from a sound sleep by a rustling or whirring sound, a very pleasant *whoosh* like a sudden breeze through tall silent grass, felt rather than heard. Suddenly David was standing at the bedside. He was already at work, urging his brother-in-law to change his ways, to dare to repent before God. David knew the importance of the heavenly system and the value of following the principles the Lord has established for man's happiness. Brent's wife hadn't heard or seen anything, but before he could be frightened or upset by such an encounter, Brent admitted that he was filled with a deep impression of David's shining *beauty* and *knowingness!* "I hope I'll remember what David said to me—it was so right! Anyway, I know I will never forget how joyful he seemed and how good I felt in his presence."

*   *   *

Lynn Anderson's friend had an experience that was sacred to her, and she shares it as follows:

"Recently I was asked to assist Mrs. Lynn Anderson in initiating a fund-raising campaign to support gene therapy research in epidermolysis bullosa. It had been a long time since

I had been involved in such an endeavor, so I began slowly with small tasks growing to greater involvement as the cause became more real and an end was in sight. Along with the practical aspects of the over-all venture, I grew to know Lynn as a kind and gentle woman but with an iron-willed determination to reach her goals. I should mention here that I was aware that Lynn and her family had sustained much sorrow in the loss of her son, Chuck, and daughter, Christine, to EB. I did not know Chuck. He had died before I entered the cosmos of the clinical and research investigations of this disease. It was Christine that I had met in the EB clinic. Even then, my personal involvement was a clinical one. Hence, as the fund-raising project grew, I enjoyed the budding of a new friendship with Lynn. With each day I came to realize that her devotion to the cause at hand revealed her dedication to the memory of her children and to finding a cure for EB children everywhere.

"Along the way something unusual happened.

"A few weeks after I became a part of the fund-raising efforts, I had a spiritual revelation. Now, I am a no-nonsense Christian person with a true faith in the goodness and love of God, but without the need for symbolism that many religions provide. I am also a life-long learning, scientifically trained investigator in medical anthropology and epidemiology— here again, a believer as well as a generator of factual data.

"One morning as I had responded to my alarm's awakening call, I stood up and headed toward the shower, and to my wonderment I saw 'something' on the wall a few feet away from me. I now call it a vision. I had never seen a vision before. In fact, I did not know what I was looking at.

"On the wall in a three-dimensional form was an image shrouded in a cloudy mist, but bright and clear-cut. Within the encircling mist I perceived the small figure to be that of Christine. She was bathed in yellow light and appeared to be wearing a yellow dress. She was smiling and reaching her arms out to me. I was not afraid or startled. It seemed quite natural. As she moved ever so slightly in a back-and-forth motion, she looked like a happy, healthy child one would see in a schoolyard. She spoke to me. There was no audible sound, but I heard her. She said, 'You are helping my mother.' I was suddenly filled with a sense of warmth that flowed throughout my body and an acute sensation of her presence. The experience lasted only moments, and she was gone.

"I was hesitant to share this experience with Lynn. I thought she might think me a nutcase. I myself did not know what to think. If it were not for the fact that I was fully awake and standing, I would have thought I had had a dream. I finally did tell Lynn of the revelation, and I am glad that I did. Far from thinking I was crazy, she was immediately drawn to the experience and queried me in detail. For the first time in our association, she told me of her own religious beliefs, and that she had wished that Christine and Chuck would one day visit her.

"This brings to me to the question: *Why* did Christine come to me, and why to *me*? I had not been a close acquaintance or involved in her medical care. I have tried over the passing weeks to ferret out a resolution to this quandry. And Christine's presence has remained with me ever since."

*　　*　　*

The incident that Mark Pehrson shared with me happened when he was driving his wife and another couple home from a dinner party. "It was just one of those things, you know?" said Mark soberly. "Road construction at a main intersection, traffic lights improperly timed to accommodate traffic flow, a driver racing through a yellow light and smashing into our car. Diane's side of the car received the brunt of the broadside hit. The impact was so horrendous that it knocked the car five hundred feet from the street into a vacant parking lot behind an empty commercial building. It was totally dark and quiet after the screeching noise of the crash.

"My first thought was for Diane. 'Are you all right, honey?' I asked, wiping the blood from my eyes with my coat sleeve, and twisting to look at her. Suddenly there was a light about her—the lights were out on the car and there were no lights on in the old parking lot, *but she had light about her face!* As I stared at her, waiting for an answer, the light became increasingly brighter until she really glowed. She had this beautiful smile and her face looked so peaceful. It was then I realized that she was gone. But there was something else—she was not alone. The car seemed crowded with personages about her. I felt them there. And there was echoing stillness, not empty silence. It was incredibly sweet. Though I wept for the loss of her companionship that I had enjoyed for many years, I was so grateful for this spiritual manifestation of angels. I knew that this had been no accident, but it had been God's will. How wonderful to be *known by God* that way! I knew that Diane was all right, and I would be too." Mark and Diane's children and grandchildren treasure this witness.

The night of the accident, Mark and Diane Pehrson had been returning from dinner at the oceanfront home of Alice, a lifelong friend. That spring day Alice had gathered blooming succulents from a hill near her home to decorate the dinner table. Now each spring when those blooms reappear and turn the field into a purple-and-white tapestry, Alice sits on the hill thinking of Diane and weeping—marveling, too, at the wondrous ways of God. She said: "He gives us joyful relationships, exquisite beauty of nature, comfort, and evidence that heaven is close. What Mark saw and felt when Diane was caught up to heaven is, I feel, sacred as well as a true witness to me."

Following our conversation, remembering the anniversary of Diane's death, Alice mailed me a moisture pack of purple and white field blossoms to confirm her feelings!

*   *   *

Brian was a discouraged young father who was financially so far behind and beleaguered with debt and worry that he had thought of nothing but suicide for weeks. He had made careful plans and that night made love to his wife for the last time in a kind of sacramental plea for her forgiveness of what he was preparing to do.

He fell fast asleep, peaceful for the first time in a long while. He was awakened by someone calling him by name. He opened his eyes to a man sitting on the side of the bed. His first thought was that he should be frightened, but an amazing feeling of well-being swept over him as the man identified himself as Brian's father. Brian had been eleven years old when his dad had died years ago. The figure of light talked quietly, gently, wisely, and pleasantly to Brian until shortly before dawn.

Brian's wife had slept through the whole visit, but when she was told about it she wept with her husband. To this day, Brian really cannot recall anything specific that his father said to him that night, nor did his father touch him in any way. "But I can recall clearly how hopeful and helpful it was and how I felt," Brian said. "It turned my life around. That was ten years ago, but it seems like yesterday. I feel his strength with me still. I am a bishop now; we're enjoying financial success and a loving family relationship. I feel this sacred experience to be a great blessing and a gift from God!"

*   *   *

The following story is about a young mother who, like most of us, wasn't perfect but surely wanted to keep on the close side of God.

Margaret was a caregiver to Joe, her invalid husband. She also had young children to provide for. She cursed the storm that delayed her getting home from work on time to pull her materials together, check on the children, and take off for a university forty-five miles away. She had a lecture to give. One more delay that really soured her mood was trying to roust her sons to get the walks shoveled before dark. She had screamed at them, lost her cool entirely—too much pressure, too heavy a load. But she *had* to work! She didn't need that kind of guilt on a night like this.

"Rats!" she exploded as the blinding storm delayed traffic. This snow was serious snowman quality, she thought to herself, as she negotiated the on ramp and began progressing across the lanes of traffic to the far left lane so that she could pick up her route south at the interchange up ahead. She had driven this stretch countless times; it was just that with the snow screen it was like trying to do it blind! She counted: first lane, second lane, third lane—or was it just the second lane? She couldn't see and she'd lost track. What if something happened to her on a night like this, feeling as she did about dumping on the boys at home? A silent but specific prayer swelled her heart, "Father, forgive me. Forgive me, please. Take care of Joe and my boys. Help me to get back safely to them. I need a chance to make it up to them. Oh, Father! We need each other and I need thee. Help me, help me."

Now her snow-clouded vision was watered by tears. Confused, Margaret flipped her blinker to signal left and move into the passing lane. At once she realized her mistake. She had gone too far! Obviously she had already been in the passing lane and was headed down the slope into the median strip.

"Oh, God, my Eternal Father," she cried out loud. Just then she felt another power wrest the wheel from her hands, and with a strength she had never had, the car was turned sharply back up the slope, through the slush and snow to the passing lane, which was miraculously free of traffic at that very moment!

Margaret was safely on her way again, trembling all over though she was. Over and over again she spoke out loud to give thanks for an answered prayer. She felt protected all the way to the university.

By the time she stood in front of her class she was mellowed. She did not tell them about her close call, nor did she try to describe her feeling about what had happened to her. She knew it was heavenly help. She hadn't *seen* anything, but that it was an angel helping her was confirmed by the tenderness of spirit that overwhelmed her through the power of the Holy Ghost.

*   *   *

The impact of Craig's snowmobile crashing into a tree immediately injured his spinal column, paralyzing his legs. Though his arms were also damaged, they were making some progress. He said, "When this happened, I was twenty-two and engaged to be married to a great girl named Jenny. Of course that fell through. I think that losing Jenny was harder than losing the use of my legs. The night she came to tell me our relationship was over was bad, bad, bad! Her parents had convinced her to break the engagement, but she admitted that she really wouldn't be good at helping me so totally forever. Well, that night my temperature shot up and Mom sent for the Elders to give me a blessing. It was really late and quiet, and the room was dark except for the small reading light behind the bed. Dad had never been a church person, but the Elders asked him to help them administer to me. During the blessing I remember wondering how my dad was taking this, so I opened my eyes and looked at him. He seemed calm and focused, but right behind him was a tall cloud or a flood of thick, white light that encircled something. I really couldn't say for sure, but I felt that it was my grandpa—Dad's father. He had been a patriarch when he was alive, and I think maybe he came to back Dad up. You know? Well, I didn't rise and walk or anything, but I'll be okay. I've had my mission; I've been in love; and I had this awesome spiritual experience. I guess that from now on, I'll just see what I can do for my dad and others. Did I tell you that nobody else in the room saw or felt anything out of the ordinary that night of the blessing? Like, wow!"

*   *   *

Steve Butler had been an alcoholic for years, much to the great distress of his loving wife and four beautiful daughters. Because he was a highly successful businessman in a job that required almost constant travel and a fast lifestyle, the drinking problem had been tolerated for many years. Every Christmas—when they all did get together from their scattered places—was repetitious heartbreak. Dad's *problem* ruined things for everybody.

Then came a season when the daughters, now with grown children themselves, reluctantly agreed to try a week-long reunion between Christmas and New Year's at the family's well-appointed ski chalet. One more time!

On the morning of Christmas Eve, Steve's drinking began in earnest. The daughters dreaded the coming hours of drunkenness. They also worried about his example before their impressionable children and teenagers. The oldest daughter, Janna, was a spiritual giant. She was one who had found her direction and purpose in life. Christmas Eve she prayed earnestly for guidance about her dad's drinking and the related family relationships. In the early hours of Christmas Day, Janna was awakened by a voice calling her name. She sat up and looked around, then noted a light in the corner that had not awakened her husband. As she looked, the light grew brighter and she saw her mother's father, Gramps, who had been dead for several years. That gentle, good man had come back to help them.

In telling the story, Janna emphasized two things—her absolute surprise and her total lack of fear. Janna never heard anything but her own name. As soon as she recognized and started to speak to Gramps, he was gone. However, the delicious, warm swelling of hope and love did not dissipate in the waning light. Janna *felt an understanding* of what she had to do. She could hardly wait for daylight so the sisters could initiate the plan to gang up on Dad.

Steve was caught off guard with the suggestion of a father-daughter "time out" early Christmas morning before brunch and gifts. What? No children allowed? No spouses? Dad and daughters skied over to a favorite spot that overlooked the ski runs of the commercial resort adjoining their acreage. Steve, of course, immediately took out his flask of liquor. The daughters were ready. This was it. Janna made him promise he'd not talk, just listen—then he could take his turn. Janna started first, and each girl had her say. They praised their father for being a good provider and working so hard at his job. They were affectionate and told him of their love. Each also told of her own concern about staying overnight in a house that would reveal drunken vulgarity and bleary-eyed interaction of Grandpa with their children. Now that Mom was alone all the time—and she was so sick of Dad's drinking—divorce was a real possibility. Tears were easy because they all felt so strongly about saving the family. Janna pointed out her dream of a Christmas season that would be a time of family sharing, tenderness, and even holiness with loving angels hovering nearby. But then Janna took courage as she held hands with her sisters and admitted that this was their last Christmas with him ever—if he didn't throw away his flask at once and never take another drink. Cold turkey! That was it! Weeping over their concern for him and because he was so ashamed, Steve did throw away his flask and keep his family. He never took another drink after that. When Janna shared their experience, she said that every Christmas she has a special "Thank you, Gramps" in her prayers for help just when she needed it most.

*   *   *

Clyn Barrus shared this story during a summer workshop on music at Brigham Young University in August 1994. "While living for several years in Vienna, Austria, Maryon and I became closely acquainted with the branch president of the First Vienna Branch. President Mieka was an unusual person. He not only served diligently in his ecclesiastical responsibilities but also recognized the power of music. One would expect the great musical capital of Vienna to produce outstanding musicians, but our little branch was only sparsely talented when it came to musical performance. We did have a small branch choir of fifteen or twenty members, with no tenors and two altos. After long, diligent, and at times discouraging rehearsals, we would perform periodically in sacrament meeting and felt grateful when our performance was not outright embarrassing. You can imagine how we felt when President Mieka came to us in September and expressed his desire to have us perform all three sections of Handel's *Messiah* at Christmastime, two and one half months later.

"The few musicians in the group, myself included, thought that President Mieka must be delirious for suggesting such an impossible task. We realized his resolve, however, when he showed us the choir music he had already purchased and indicated that he had budgeted eight hundred shillings (thirty-two dollars) from the ward budget to hire a small orchestra and whatever soloists were not available in the ward. *Not available in the ward!* We were lucky to have a soprano who could carry a tune, let alone sing a solo that would be recognizable. There was, however, no way to convince President Mieka that his request was impossible, and we began the grueling task of trying to fulfill his wishes.

"Through the coming weeks significant blessings came to us. Dr. Alma Dittmer, who taught music at Ricks College and at Utah State University for many years, came to Vienna on a semester sabbatical. He generously helped prepare our struggling choir (now increased to fifty members) and offered to sing the bass solos. We were able to convince an inactive member who was also a well-known alto soloist in Vienna to sing with us, and a fine soprano who was a member of the Church came to Vienna to study music at the academy. One of the members knew a well-trained tenor soloist and convinced him to complete our solo quartet.

"By the first of December I had lined up a string quartet from the Vienna Academy to join with the organ to create our tiny orchestra, and our final rehearsals began. The state of our preparation was best described when a close friend and member of the string quartet came to me during our final rehearsal and whispered in my ear. 'We're not going to make it, are we?' I put my arm around him and said, 'Of course we will,' but realized he may be right. We worked hard and long trying to prepare this gigantic masterpiece. People who had only sung simple hymn melodies were struggling with the complex melismatic phrases that are so prevalent in the *Messiah*. Others simply could not read music and were singing totally by ear. They had given every ounce of their dedication and large amounts of time to prepare for this performance.

"Sunday before Christmas is an important part of the religious worship in Austria. Most Americans attended a midnight mass, even if they had never visited another church service during the years. President Mieka scheduled our performance of the *Messiah* on that Sunday evening at seven o'clock so that it would be completed in time for nonmembers to attend later services. He then asked the entire elders quorum of the branch to distribute fliers throughout the area of Vienna surrounding the church building.

"Handel's *Messiah* is not sung with regularity in German-speaking countries, even though Handel was German by birth. Translating scripture from one language to another with musical cohesiveness is very difficult and is at times awkward. One Jewish member felt the German translation of the *Messiah* recalled too closely the salutation given to Adolf

Hitler just twenty years earlier. He sang in spite of his concern.

"The unfamiliarity but strong reputation of the *Messiah* brought an enormous crowd of music-loving Viennese to our concert. As the crowd grew in size, the hearts of our poor choir shriveled, and some seriously considered heading to the nearest exit. Our trembling was climaxed when two full rows of priests and nuns from the neighboring Catholic church entered our chapel. Clergy of the Catholic church do not normally enter buildings of other denominations, and as we looked at them we imagined written on their faces, 'This had better be good.'

"The concert began with President Mieka's warm welcome and assurance of the quality of the performance—in spite of the fact that he sang bass in the choir and knew well the limits of our ability. He then offered a prayer, most of which I still remember in detail. He asked the Lord to touch the hearts of the choir and other performers. He said that we do this not for ourselves but because of our desire to testify to all present of the life and mission of Jesus Christ, our Savior. He then prayed, 'Oh Lord, we are inadequate to express our testimony through this masterwork without thy presence. We ask thee to send angels from heaven to stand at our side and sing this message with us—that we may bear not only in spirit but in actuality the heavenly choirs of which the scriptures speak.' The sincerity of his prayer was so powerful that, though we may not have seen the angels, we felt and heard their presence at our side as we sang praises to our Lord.

"At the conclusion of the performance, the audience sat

in solemn silence. They had been deeply moved as the Spirit of our Father in Heaven touched their hearts. 'No tongue can speak, neither can there be written by any man, neither can the hearts of men conceive so great and marvelous things as we both saw and heard. . . .'[3] It was one of the most significant musical and spiritual experiences of my life."

*   *   *

Angels are in our midst in other ways than with music. The story of Peggy and Jarvis shows how angels can keep someone from self-destruction. Peggy and Jarvis each came from good heritage and tried to live according to gospel principles. Of course, like the rest of us, they were not perfect—but they wanted to be. They had fallen in love, married, and then had three children in stair-step style. Then came the twins. They brought hearts full of joy to their parents, but what a challenge! The struggle was financial as well as emotional and physical for two people learning to live together in love.

Then Jarvis accepted a sales job with immediate financial benefits, and they felt on top of all happiness. However, the job required that Jarvis travel nearly twenty-five days out of every month. Peggy began to wear down from the burden of being, practically speaking, a single parent. Besides, she had a garden to keep and an enormous laundry and household chore schedule, and she helped out at church.

One day Peggy reached her lowest ebb.

It was her birthday. Jarvis was out of town, of course.

How would she celebrate? Bitterly she thought about it. "Oh, I know, I will celebrate by painting the nursery." Jarvis had put it off since the promise he made to her when the twins were born. Well, she'd show him! Peggy climbed a ladder, bitterly singing, "Happy birthday to you, Peggy," and began splashing on paint to the tune of self-pity. The more this went on, the more destructive her thinking became. She thought about plans for *bolting this trap.* She seriously considered hiring a sitter for the children and simply escaping with a new identity. The thought of leaving the twin babies brought forth fresh sobbing. But now she cried because she was ashamed; next she cried out to God for help. Suddenly, she felt warm arms of love encircle her. She gasped, thinking Jarvis had surprised her by coming home and had climbed the ladder below her to hug her. She turned her head to greet him and saw nothing, though she still felt the warm hug that comforted her. She knew that God had heard her prayers, and she was strengthened beyond any expectation.

*   *   *

When we are in trouble and are reassured that God lives and is aware of our tragedy—especially through sending angels to help—life's trials are not only more endurable but also tinged with unsuspected blessings and purpose.

Angels in our midst confirm God's existence and underscore his love for each of us. Our challenge is to keep faithful so that we may be in a position for the further and unspeakable joy that he has promised.

NOTES

1. Hebrews 13:2.
2. See Doctrine and Covenants 130:1–2.
3. 3 Nephi 17:17.

Three

ANGELS
ROUND ABOUT YOU

*E*arly one day "as the light of the morning [came] out of the east, and [shined] even unto the west"[1] beyond Utah Lake, just past the time of a golden dawn breaking over Mount Timpanogos yet still firing the spire of the Provo Temple, I watched the gates of the Missionary Training Center swing open. Overwhelmed, I gloried in the stream of missionaries flooding forth toward the temple up the hill. They are at a marvelous peak in life—young, beautiful, vigorous, animated, and serious about their new focus. They are full of a divine spirit and light that will shine across the whole world, wherever their field of service may be. This awesome sight is reminiscent of the 1832 season of joy in Kirtland, Ohio, when the brethren of the Restoration began returning from the first missions elated and elevated.

There is more. These set-apart servants are buoyant, as if

angels round about are ushering them along a sacred corridor. *Angel* means messenger; missionaries are themselves mortal angels.

To every missionary the Lord has said that he sends his servants forth to reprove the world of their unrighteous deeds and to teach of an inevitable judgment.[2] Furthermore, "Whoso receiveth you, there I will be also, for I will go before your face. I will be on your right hand and on your left, and my Spirit shall be in your hearts, and mine angels round about you, to bear you up."[3]

Remarkable events take place with the *bearing up* that comes when angels are round about and minister. This chapter contains honest, unvarnished, and inspiring experiences about the ministering of angels to prophets and ordinary people alike.

For example, at the time of Christ's birth, ministry, and death on one continent, another continent in the western hemisphere was plagued by governments being overthrown by citizens divided among themselves. A man called Nephi became a messenger of repentance and faith in Christ. So powerful was his faith in the Lord Jesus Christ that angels did abound about him and ministered to him daily! He even raised his own dead brother, who had been stoned by wicked people who resented his preaching.[4]

Another example concerns Amaleki, who entrusted the sacred records of their people to Benjamin, also a man of God. On that occasion Amaleki exhorted all men "to come unto God, the Holy One of Israel, and believe in prophesying, and in revelations, *and in the ministering of angels*."[5]

David A. Smith served as first counselor to Elder Sylvester Q. Cannon in the Presiding Bishopric of the Church and was a man who wholeheartedly accepted the things of God. In 1923 he spoke with full spirit at the dedication of the Alberta Temple in Canada. He explained how much he had loved his deceased father, President Joseph F. Smith. David told of his longing to visit with his father about the matters of the kingdom and to enjoy his spiritual guidance and companionship. Then he testified: "Yesterday I walked with him in these halls, . . . [and again] by his side I stood while offering up the sacred shout of Hosanna."[6]

Many, including three Presidents of the Church, have told a ministering angel story in the family of Bishop John Wells. President Ezra Taft Benson spoke of it as follows:

"A son of Bishop and Sister Wells was killed in a railroad accident on October 15, 1915. He was run over by a freight car. Sister Wells could not be consoled. She received no comfort during the funeral and continued her mourning after her son was laid to rest. Bishop Wells feared for her health, as she was in a state of deep anguish.

"One day, soon after the funeral, Sister Wells was lying on her bed in a state of mourning. The son appeared to her and said, 'Mother, do not mourn, do not cry. I am all right.'

"He then related to her how the accident took place. Apparently there had been some question—even suspicion—about the accident because the young man was an experienced railroad man. But he told his mother that it was clearly an accident.

"Now note this: He also told her that as soon as he

realized that he was in another sphere, he had tried to reach his father but could not. His father was so busy with the details of his office and work that he could not respond to the promptings. Therefore, the son had come to his mother.

"He then said, 'Tell Father that all is well with me, and I want you not to mourn any more.' "[7]

A very remarkable moment honored Elder LeGrand Richards in the later years of his life as an Apostle. Giving the priesthood to all worthy male members of the Church, regardless of race, had been a major consideration for many years. Most people had very strong feelings about the issue. During a dramatic meeting guided by President Spencer W. Kimball, during which the issue was being deeply discussed, Elder Richards suddenly felt a warm, spiritual flush over his entire body. His heart began to beat faster. He was aware that there was an angel in the room and recognized the late prophet Wilford Woodruff sitting among them! In his day President Woodruff had wrestled with the painful challenge of the Church's practice of polygamy being a deterrent to statehood for the Utah territory. He finally delivered the Manifesto, which ended the Church's practice of polygamy in 1890.

At first Elder Richards was reluctant to share what he had seen and felt, but when he did, the quorum solemnly agreed that the appearance of President Woodruff was a glorious sign of support to the Brethren gathered in the temple. Elder Richards then added that he believed he had been privileged to actually see the vision because he was the only one present old enough to have known President Woodruff while he was alive.[8]

President Spencer W. Kimball believed in angelic help and frequently referred to the ministering of angels. He wrote: "I am sure that the veil is thin. My grandfather, being one of a family, searched all his life to get together his genealogical records; and when he died in 1868, he had been unsuccessful in establishing his line back more than the second generation beyond him. I am sure that most of my family members feel the same as I do—that there was a thin veil between him and the earth, after he had gone to the other side, and that which he was unable to do as a mortal he perhaps was able to do after he had gone into eternity. After he passed away, the spirit of research suddenly took hold of [family members] in the West and two distant relatives, not members of the Church, in the East. For seven years these two men—Morrison and Sharples—unknown to each other, and unknown to the members of the family in the West, were gathering genealogy. After seven years, they happened to meet and then for three years they worked together. The family feels definitely that the Spirit of Elijah was at work on the other side and that our grandfather had been able to inspire men on this side to search out these records, and as a result, two large volumes are in our possession with about seventeen thousand names!"[9]

President Harold B. Lee shared one of his sacred experiences during general conference, April 8, 1973. I include this here in the hope that it can help others identify the source of their own angelic ministrations.

"May I impose upon you for a moment to express appreciation for something that happened to me some time ago. I was suffering from an ulcer condition that was becoming worse and worse. We had been touring a mission; my wife, Joan, and I were impressed the next morning that we should get home as quickly as possible, although we had planned to stay for some other meetings.

"On the way across the country, we were sitting in the forward section of the airplane. Some of our Church members were in the next section. As we approached a certain point en route, someone laid his hand upon my head. I looked up; I could see no one. That happened again before we arrived home, again with the same experience. Who it was, by what means or what medium, I may never know, except I knew that I was receiving a blessing that I came a few hours later to know I needed most desperately.

"As soon as we arrived home, my wife very anxiously called the doctor. It was now about eleven o'clock at night. He called me to come to the telephone, and asked how I was; and I said, 'Well, I am very tired. I think I will be all right.' But shortly thereafter, there came massive hemorrhages which, had they occurred while we were in flight, I wouldn't be here today talking about it.

"I know that there are powers divine that reach out when all other help is not available."[10]

Many may have heard the following experience included in the papers and speeches of President David O. McKay. It was most sacred to him and should be to us because the prophecy stated herein has been fulfilled.

"I was on my first mission, president, at the time, of the Scottish conference in the year 1899. Presiding over the European Mission were Elders Platt D. Lyman, Henry W. Naisbitt, and James L. McMurrin. President McMurrin represented the European Mission presidency at a conference held in Glasgow, Scotland. Following a series of meetings, we held a most remarkable priesthood meeting—one that will never be forgotten by any who was present.

"I remember as if it were but yesterday, the intensity of the inspiration of that occasion. Everybody felt the rich outpouring of the Spirit of the Lord. All present were truly of one heart and one mind. Never before had I experienced such an emotion. It was a manifestation for which as a doubting youth I had secretly prayed most earnestly on hillside and in meadow. It was an assurance to me that sincere prayer is answered 'sometime, somewhere.'

"During the progress of the meeting, an elder on his own initiative arose and said, 'Brethren, there are angels in this room.' Strange as it may seem, the announcement was not startling; indeed, it seemed wholly proper; though it had not occurred to me there were divine beings present. I only knew that I was overflowing with gratitude for the presence of the Holy Spirit. I was profoundly impressed, however, when President James L. McMurrin arose and confirmed that statement by pointing to one brother sitting just in front of me and saying, 'Yes, brethren, there are angels in this room, and one of them is the guardian angel of that young man sitting there,' and he designated one who today is a patriarch of the Church.

"Pointing to another elder, he said, 'And one is the guardian angel of that young man there,' and he singled out one whom I had known from childhood. Tears were rolling down the cheeks of both of these missionaries, not in sorrow or grief, but as an expression of the overflowing Spirit; indeed, we were all weeping.

"Such was the setting in which James L. McMurrin gave what has since proved to be a prophecy. I had learned by intimate association with him that James McMurrin was pure gold; his faith in the gospel implicit; that no truer man, no more loyal man to what he thought was right ever lived; so when he turned to me and gave what I thought was more of a caution than a promise, his words made an indelible impression upon me. Paraphrasing the words of the Savior to Peter, he said, 'Let me say to you, Brother David, Satan hath desired you that he may sift you as wheat, but God is mindful of you.' Then he added, 'If you will keep the faith, you will yet sit in the leading councils of the Church.' "[11]

President Gordon B. Hinckley has had a life of sacred experiences and great spiritual tutoring. His words should be listened to and meditated on for the good of all. He referred specifically to young men who hold the Aaronic Priesthood as "these boys here, who are in this hall today, who have received that Aaronic Priesthood and who are entitled, if they live for the blessings, to receive the ministering of angels, the guidance of the Spirit, the protecting power of the Lord in their lives."[12]

On another occasion President Hinckley said: "I desire to impress upon you the fact that it does not make any difference whether a man is a Priest or an Apostle if he magnifies his calling. . . . A priest holds the keys of the ministering of angels. 'Never in my life,' said President Woodruff, 'as an Apostle, as a Seventy, or as an Elder, have I ever had more of the protection of the Lord than while holding the office of a Priest. The Lord revealed to me by visions, by revelations, and by the Holy Spirit many things that lay before me.' "[13]

How blessed we are to have the testimony of President Gordon B. Hinckley to underscore the truth about angels: "I add my testimony that Joseph was and is the great prophet of this dispensation of the fulness of times, that he was raised up by the God of heaven, that he was tutored and directed by the risen Lord Jesus Christ and also by angels who were sent from the heavens to restore the everlasting priesthood with all of its powers and keys to reestablish the Church of Jesus Christ in the earth and to set in motion a cause and kingdom that will spread to every nation, kindred, tongue, and people."[14]

Angels represent God and serve as they are assigned among mortals. Some people in sacred circumstances have recognized those who have died and then returned to earth as angels for some good purpose. Dean Jarman, a stake president, wrote: "The question can now be asked if there is a specific guardian angel assigned to each individual? There is nothing in the scriptures that suggests this to be the case . . . there is no evidence of a guardian angel assigned to every person; but angels have served a guardian role as they warn, protect, and strengthen those they have ministered to on earth."[15] Elder John A. Widtsoe cast a further dimension as follows: "The common belief . . . that to every person born into the world is assigned a guardian angel to be with that

THE TRUTH ABOUT ANGELS

person constantly, is not supported by available evidence. . . .
In fact, the constant presence of the Holy Ghost would seem
to make such a constant, angelic companionship unnecessary."[16] According to Elder Bruce R. McConkie, "To suppose that either all men or all righteous men have heavenly
beings acting as guardians for them runs counter to the basic
revealed facts relative to the manner in which the Lord exercises his benevolent watchfulness over his mortal men."[17]

Some people are so hungry for spiritual experiences that
they want to hear the Brethren speak of them openly in public broadcasts such as general conference or other gatherings
where nonmembers or nonbelievers are in attendance. Sensitive people to whom angels have ministered are usually God-
loving and God-honoring. Not only are they disinterested in
media attention or public acclaim for such sacred experiences,
they abhor it. Because of skeptics and those who would treat
heavenly matters lightly, speaking publicly about ministering
angels should be done with great sensitivity. Speaking of sacred things is appropriate only when moved upon by the
Holy Ghost, because God's angels are round about to bear
up his mortal servants and such events are held sacred.

NOTES

1. Joseph Smith—Matthew 1:26.
2. See Doctrine and Covenants 84:87.

3. Doctrine and Covenants 84:88.

4. See 3 Nephi 7:17–19.

5. Omni 1:25; emphasis added.

6. Summary of Alberta Dedication Addresses, Susa Young Gates Papers, Utah State Historical Society, p. 233.

7. Ezra Taft Benson, "Seek the Spirit of the Lord," *Ensign,* April 1988, p. 2.

8. See *Deseret News,* 15 January 1983, p. B2. This event was confirmed both by members of Elder LeGrand Richards's family and by Elder Boyd K. Packer in his remarks at Elder Richards's funeral.

9. Edward L. Kimball, ed., *The Teachings of Spencer W. Kimball* (Salt Lake City: Bookcraft, 1982), p. 543.

10. Harold B. Lee, *The Teachings of Harold B. Lee* (Salt Lake City: Bookcraft, 1996), p. 491.

11. David O. McKay, in Conference Report, October 1968, p. 86.

12. Gordon B. Hinckley, in Vacaville–Santa Rosa Regional Conference, 21 May 1995.

13. Gordon B. Hinckley, in Boston Regional Conference, Priesthood Leadership Session, 22 April 1995.

14. Gordon B. Hinckley, "A Wonderful Summer," in *Brigham Young University 1989–90 Devotional and Fireside Speeches* (Provo, Utah: University Publications, 1990), p. 15.

15. Dean Jarman, in "Q and A," *New Era,* September 1983, p. 50.

16. John A. Widtsoe, *Evidences and Reconciliations,* comp. G. Homer Durham (Salt Lake City: Bookcraft, 1960), p. 403.

17. Bruce R. McConkie, *Mormon Doctrine,* 2nd ed. (Salt Lake City: Bookcraft, 1960), p. 341.

Four

GOD CREATED
ANGELS

*K*ing Benjamin's deathbed counsel to his beloved
people in ancient America would be classic in any era. His ad-
vice for happiness and full living is still relevant today and
contains basic truths upon which everything else hinges: "Believe in God; believe that he is, and that he created all things,
both in heaven and in earth" and that people cannot "comprehend all the things which the Lord can comprehend."[1]

King Benjamin knew and taught what every prophet of
God in every dispensation has taught—that God is the creator of all things: God created all the children of men in
heaven before there was "flesh upon the earth, neither in the
water, neither in the air."[2] What can be more clear than the
fact that all things are spiritually created before they take a
place on earth?

God himself explained that he was the "Great I AM,

Alpha and Omega, the beginning and the end, the same which looked upon the wide expanse of all eternity, and all the seraphic hosts of heaven, before the world was made."[3] Angels were present at the time of the war in heaven when the plans for this earth were under discussion.

Angels are part of the whole heavenly family, as mortals are. Angels and mortals are simply God's children at different stages of the total experience in heaven and on earth. Those of God's spiritual creations who are *in his image* and retained their first estate eventually come to earth for a turn to live and die. Everyone! The agenda and timetable for each Godlike spirit is unique along its path of progression from premortal life through earth life and through all eternity. The essence or intelligence of man is self-existent and with God in the beginning when God organized the very elements of creation.[4]

Brigham Young said, "How gladly would we understand every principle pertaining to science and art, and become thoroughly acquainted with every intricate operation of nature, and with all the chemical changes that are constantly going on around us! How delightful this would be, and what a boundless field of truth and power is open for us to explore! We are only just approaching the shores of the vast nothing of that which pertains to the heavens, to angels and celestial beings, to the place of their habitation, to the manner of their life, and their progress to still high degrees of perfection."[5]

Some years after these thoughts from Brigham Young, the prophet Joseph F. Smith had a vision which he shared in general conference, October 4, 1918. He had been pondering and praying about the Lord's visit to the spirit world while the body of Jesus was still in the tomb. In response to his pleadings before God, President Smith had received heavenly communication over a period of several months, which resulted in the revelation now contained in Doctrine and Covenants 138. This is an important source explaining the premortal preparation of spirits; it can also be comforting to those who have buried loved ones.

God created angels. We do not comprehend exactly how he did so, but with God nothing is impossible—all things have a wise and holy purpose. The truth about angels, for example, is wonderful to consider and in keeping with the Lord's self-explained mission: "For behold, this is my work and my glory—to bring to pass the immortality and eternal life of man."[6] Let there be no doubt: God created angels, and he sends angels for the good of mankind.

The work of angels reflects their individuality and preparation; God knows well how and when they can serve best. This is also true of us mortals. Not all of us have the same gifts, nor can they be of the same use to Deity and mankind. One can teach the word, another is given exceedingly great faith to heal; another is compassionate, another merciful; another has expertise in righting wrongs, in scientific advancement, in creating beauty. Some have the gift of "the beholding of angels and ministering spirits."[7]

One of the most lucid explanations—a word picture, really—about the shaping or preparation of the individual spirit, male and female, in the spirit state prior to earth life was written by Elder Bruce R. McConkie. "Being subject to law, and having their agency, all the [male and female] spirits

. . . while yet in the Eternal Presence developed aptitudes, talents, capacities, and abilities of every kind, sort and degree. During the long expanse of life which then was, an infinite variety of talents and abilities came into being. As the ages rolled, no two spirits remained alike. Mozart became a musician. Einstein centered his interest in mathematics, Michelangelo turned his attention to painting. Cain was a liar, a schemer, a rebel who maintained a close affinity to Lucifer. Abraham and Moses and all of the prophets sought and obtained a talent for spirituality. Mary and Eve were two of the greatest of all the spirit daughters of the Father. The whole house of Israel, known and segregated out from their fellows, was inclined toward spiritual things. And so it went through all the hosts of heaven, each individual developing such talents and abilities as his soul desired."[8]

There are those who at this time are unembodied spirits. They have not as yet been given a mortal body and a turn on earth, but that turn will come as part of the plan of salvation established for all of God's spirit children, except the third part of the hosts of heaven who followed Satan.

Others have passed through mortal life and experienced death. They are disembodied spirits awaiting resurrection, when the body and the soul are united again. Some angels are translated beings who have not tasted death. They too wait for resurrection's change that provides for life ever after.

To illustrate this principle, allow an example taken from among God's creations, the species of the *cecropia moth,* a bat-sized creature whose metamorphosis is a type and shadow of the very thing we have been talking about. This moth begins in an egg deposited along a thick twig by the female moth. The egg hatches into a fat caterpillar, which matures to build a cocoon in which it will pupate. This means that within that cocoon, the caterpillar goes through a total change. It becomes an elegant creature who can fly rather than crawl and grovel for existence. In the final stage, the cecropia moth eats its way out of its own cocoon and immediately takes wing![9] What an amazing Creator we worship!

NOTES

1. Mosiah 4:9.

2. Moses 3:5.

3. Doctrine and Covenants 38:1.

4. See Joseph Smith, *Teachings of the Prophet Joseph Smith,* comp. Joseph Fielding Smith (Salt Lake City: Deseret Book Co., 1976), pp. 353–54.

5. Brigham Young, in *Journal of Discourses* 9:168.

6. Moses 1:39.

7. Moroni 10:14.

8. Bruce R. McConkie, *The Mortal Messiah,* vol. 1. (Salt Lake City: Deseret Book Co., 1979), p. 23.

9. *Smithsonian,* February 1996, p. 72.

Five

WHAT IS THE TRUTH ABOUT ANGELS?

*S*o what is the truth about angels? What are their vital statistics? How about wings and halos and clothing? Are there male and female angels? What is their time frame and where do they live? Can they talk? Do they have names? These are questions that often come from scoffers who try to debunk the existence of angels. Some just forget or ignore what they might have been taught. As Nephi said to his murmuring older brother, "How is it that ye have not hearkened unto the word of the Lord? How is it that ye have forgotten that ye have seen an angel of the Lord?"[1]

There are answers. There is proof. There is scriptural documentation and personal testimony from valid authority. The truth about angels is satisfying and brings infinitely more comfort than an inanimate sculpture of a winged figure or a pleasant plastic form decorating the bulletin board by your desk.

What Do Angels Look Like?

To learn what God's angels really look like, most of us must depend on someone else's view, faith and God's purposes being what they are. Just because we haven't seen our great-great-ancestors does not mean they do not exist somewhere! Limited angel statistics are available from people who have seen them and from God's own revealed words. Now, what do we know about what angels look like?

One night, right here in America, a teenage boy named Joseph Smith saw an angel as an answer to prayer—and he was nothing like the way the world portrayed them. There were no enormous wings nor opulent pastel layers of diaphanous flounces, no rounded cheeks nor dimpled hands, no sparkling halo suspended above its head. Joseph's vision was portentous for a lot of reasons. A close examination of his own description of this angel peaks our interest now:

> Immediately a personage appeared at my bedside, standing in the air, for his feet did not touch the floor. He had on a loose robe of most exquisite whiteness. It was a whiteness beyond anything earthly I had ever seen; nor do I believe any earthly thing could be made to appear so exceedingly white and brilliant. His hands were naked, and his arms also, a little above the wrist; so, also, were his feet naked, as were his legs, a little above the ankles. His head and neck were also bare. I could discover that he had no other clothing on but this robe, as it was open, so that I could see into his bosom. Not only was his robe exceedingly white, but his whole person was glorious beyond description, and his countenance truly like lightning. The room

was exceedingly light, but not so very bright as immediately around his person. . . . After . . . I saw the light in the room begin to gather immediately around the person of him who had been speaking to me, . . . I saw, as it were, a conduit open right up into heaven, and he ascended till he entirely disappeared, and the room was left as it had been before this heavenly light had made its appearance.[2]

A few years later Joseph recorded another description of an angel. This time his prayers had been to ask forgiveness for weaknesses. Through his faith and humility, Joseph felt forgiven because God ministered unto him by an "holy angel, whose countenance was as lightning, and whose garments were pure and white above all other whiteness."[3] The angel then gave Joseph power from on high to translate the language etched on the metal plates hidden by Moroni.

The very first chapter of the Book of Mormon includes Father Lehi's spiritual experiences with a pillar of fire coming to rest on a rock—thus he learned sacred things that caused him to tremble and quake. Then he saw God sitting upon his throne surrounded with "numberless concourses of angels" in the comforting human form of singing and praising God. He also saw one descending out of the midst of heaven whose "luster was above the sun at noon-day." Then twelve others appeared whose brightness did exceed that of a whole firmament full of stars.[4]

Yet another description of an angel is found in the book of Daniel. King Nebuchadnezzar, in a rage, had ordered Shadrach, Meshach, and Abednego bound and cast into a fiery furnace because they refused to bow down and worship the golden icon set up on the plain outside of Babylon. The king and many people came to see the men burned in the roaring flames. As they gleefully watched, suddenly a fourth figure brighter than the hot flames became visible! The bound men were unbound! They walked about in the midst of the fire with the fourth figure. Upon their release, it was noted that they had "no hurt," nor was an "hair of their head singed," neither was their clothing, nor had "the smell of fire had passed on them." For the king, seeing was believing! "Blessed be the God of Shadrach, Meshach, and Abed-nego," the converted man praised. "[He] hath sent his angel, and delivered his servants that trusted in him."[5]

In truth, angels look like themselves. Each is a unique personality and a forever intelligence as we are—the mix of matter, one-of-a-kind just as in the mortal state. Remember, angels and mortals are on different rungs of the ladder of life—premortal, mortal, eternal. Some of Heavenly Father's children are more full of light than others. Some have not taken up an earthly body yet. Some have lived and died and moved on through the veil. Some have been resurrected. Imagine! No more pain; no more fumbling old age with its accompanying, annoying deterioration!

What About the Gender of Angels?

There are male angels and female angels. The spirit children of Heavenly Father were created in the beginning as male or female, and they remain so. Wherever they are along the path of personal progress, they are able to move forward in an orderly fashion according to their own gender and time frame, whether as preparing premortals, mortals on earth, or postmortal beings.

Zechariah had a vision of angels that is rare in recorded scripture, for he refers to female angels and to wings. Zechariah lifted up his eyes and saw "two women, and the wind was in their wings."[6] However, biblical scholars generally believe that messengers from God to his prophets are male angels. Being on official errand for God as his servants—whether in heaven or on earth—is often the function of worthy priesthood holders. The angel who repeatedly awakened Zechariah and gave instructions on how to finish "the house of the Lord" was on an errand from God to a prophet, and, as scripture reveals their conversational exchange, Zechariah refers to the angel as *he*.

A spiritual experience with a loved one who has passed away could be recognized, and appropriately so, as either male or female. Surely grieving children have been comforted by deceased mothers. Certainly there is a mother in heaven, as Eliza R. Snow knew and taught in her poetry. And absolutely a widow left to rear several children can receive the comforting presence of their deceased father—still a male, still their father.

Male and female, evidence abounds for daily comfort that angels are in our midst.

Do Angels Have Wings?

According to the Lord's word in Doctrine and Covenants, angels' wings are a representation of power.[7] Across cultural and theological traditions in every corner of the earth, the idea of the form of angels has persisted—they look like humans, and wings were added to symbolize power and movement from heaven to earth and back, and to differentiate an angel from a person in paintings. Depicting angels with wings in religious art has been traced back to the early Christian church in about 300 A.D., with Constantine and Helena investing their vast fortunes in the building of churches and furnishing them with artifacts.

Some accounts mention a "whirring or rustling" sound accompanying an angel visit. According to those who have been awakened by "something" or been "carried" away themselves in a spiritual experience, there is definitely some kind of energy at work. The Holy Day of Pentecost with Peter was a "rushing mighty wind."[8]

During an address by George A. Smith at the dedication of the Kirtland Temple, nearly one thousand people suddenly heard a noise like the sound of a "rushing mighty wind," which filled the new temple. Being moved upon by an invisible power, all in attendance rose simultaneously.[9] Joseph Smith then explained from the pulpit that the building was filled with angels, and many people of the neighborhood outside the building came running upon hearing an unusual sound within the building. They also saw an incredibly bright light like a pillar of fire resting on the roof. All were astonished. In a sermon to the Twelve within that temple, Joseph spoke about the nature of spiritual beings and clarified, "An angel of God never has wings."[10]

In Genesis 28, we read about fine Jacob, whom the Lord described elsewhere as one "did none other things" than that which was commanded in heaven.[11] Jacob had a vision of a ladder set up on the earth, with the top of it reaching to heaven with the angels of God ascending and descending on it. No winged angels here, but rather clamoring examples of the symbolic steps all must take to reach the kingdom of heaven. The fascinating result of this vision was that Jacob was compelled to make a vow. Since God was so generous with him, he, Jacob, would give back to God a tenth of his increase. And tithing was instituted![12]

People who can grasp the wonder and import that God created all things will not be satisfied with mortal conjectures and speculations about angels. In much the same way as children confusing Santa with Jesus, or angels with fairy godmothers (however well-meaning and passionate one's own creative pondering, writing, or painting of angels may be), our understanding the truth is far more exciting and comforting. It is so important, in fact, that it should be sought after diligently.

Do Angels Have Names?

That angels have had names since the beginning is verified by scriptures such as this: "Now there was a day when the

53

sons of God came to present themselves before the Lord, and Satan came also among them."[13] According to Henri Casilles: "For the ancients a name is not simply a conventional designation, but rather an expression of a being's place in the universe."[14] Names often have reference to an angel's role at the moment; a man named Jim Cannon, for example, is called Bishop rather than Jim long after that assignment is over. When Peter taught that Christ himself had done a holy work preaching to the spirits in prison, Peter said that after Christ had gone into heaven to be on God's right hand, "angels and authorities [titles, names, office] and power [were] made subject unto him."[15]

The most oft-mentioned angel names in the Bible are Michael, who we know was Adam during his earth life, and Gabriel, who was known as the great prophet Noah on earth. New names seem to be a meaningful part of God's system. For example, Abram became Abraham; Sarah became Sariah; Saul, Paul; Jacob, Israel; and so forth. When Moses came to earth to confer keys to Joseph Smith, he identified himself as Moses, as did Peter, James, John, and Moroni. Resurrected beings seem to be chosen often to do angelic work and act as messengers from God to his prophet on earth.

One remarkable situation with respect to angels and names concerns the Three Nephites. When Christ was bidding farewell to the people in ancient America, whom he had been giving the gospel, three of his disciples expressed a desire to keep living in order to behold all the Father's doings unto the children of men until the end of earth's time. Jesus touched each one and "they came as the angels of God," who would never have pain while they dwelled in the flesh. While making a record of this, Nephi was commanded by God not to record the names of these three so that they might be "hid from the world" to serve in their special anonymous way.[16] They could help God and his children, and Satan would have no power over them. If they pray unto the Father in the name of Jesus, they can show themselves even today to whatsoever person on earth might have need. In this state they will remain until the judgment day of Christ. At that time another great change in them will occur in a twinkling of an eye so that they never taste of death as we know it. They will simply be received into the kingdom of the Father.

A number of family records of Latter-day Saints include Three Nephite experiences. While rarely are such instances shared publicly today, Paul's statement about people entertaining angels unawares is still relevant.[17] I can so testify. Now note this wonderful reference where Mormon himself speaks of angels, "I have seen them, and they have ministered unto us."[18]

Can Angels Speak?

Angels do speak, and they say the most rewarding things! Perhaps you recall a favorite scripture of mine, "The angel said: Behold, the Lord hath heard the prayers of his people."[19] Since the Lord loves all of his children, if such a blessing can come to some, it can come to others.

God created angels and he created them to speak: "I, the

Lord God, . . . send forth angels to declare . . . repentance and redemption."[20]

"Angels speak by the power of the Holy Ghost; wherefore, they speak the words of Christ," and the words of Christ tell us all things to do.[21]

Angels can speak to mortals in any language so that they can be understood—people everywhere of all tongues have purpose in life and require God's guidance.

Angels speak to proclaim the glad tidings of the gospel. We are told that the voices of Michael, Raphael, and divers angels down to the present join in praising God.[22]

Angels by the tomb of Christ spoke to the grieving Mary when she arrived on the scene: "Woman, why weepest thou? whom seekest thou?" Having heard the angels, Mary turned and saw Jesus—though not yet resurrected, still he could speak to her.[23] Widows over the ages are comforted by the thought of conversing with their own lost loves, let alone the Lord Jesus, who is no respecter of persons.

Angels enhanced King Benjamin's oratory so that his final address to the people was a forever success! Admirably, King Benjamin gave credit where it was due for the effectiveness and content of that final address on earth. He explained that the things he talked about were made known to him by an angel from God. While he had been sleeping, an angel had come and said, "Awake!" The king awoke and saw the angel in front of him. The angel spoke again, "Awake, and hear the words which I shall tell thee; for behold, I am come to declare unto you the glad tidings of great joy."[24] This was about 125 years before the birth of Christ, but Benjamin learned of that coming sacred event and shared it with his people.

Angelic power from God brought such a change to two young missionaries named for their ancestors Lehi and Nephi that their whole countenance changed; the people saw this and heard them "speak forth marvelous words." Then a voice came to them—a pleasant voice as if it were a whisper—that blessed them with peace because of their faith. Then the heavens opened and "angels came down out of heaven and ministered" to the three hundred astonished and joyous people. They were told by angels to go forth and doubt not![25]

What Is the Time and Place of Angels?

Here is a singular statement that people generally overlook when they think about angels. "Is not the reckoning of God's time, angel's time, prophet's time, and man's time, according to the planet on which they reside?"[26] Think about that in terms of the international, ongoing debate among scientists and theologians about whether there is life on other planets in any other universe, for example!

Gabriel announced to both Elizabeth and Mary their missions as mothers. But note what information is included in his message to Zacharias: "I am Gabriel [his new name], that stand in the presence of God; and am sent to speak unto thee, and to shew thee these glad tidings."[27] He gave his name and told where he lived, whom he served, and why he had come. Then he warned Zacharias that if he did not believe what God had in mind for Sariah that Zacharias would be struck dumb. And he was! Let that be a fresh lesson for one who yearns for an angel visit or is honored with one by surprise. The key words are *believe, trust, obey,* and *remember* that with God nothing is impossible.

Joseph Smith is the classic example of the principle taught in James 1:5. When he wanted further light and knowledge, Joseph asked God and amazing truth flooded him. Later, questions would arise in his mind while he was translating the Book of Mormon or preparing a sermon to the Saints. On one occasion while Joseph was prayerfully translating, that same Moroni—who centuries before had hidden up the plates according to a commandment from God and had come back as a resurrected angel to show Joseph where they were hidden—returned again in answer to another prayer and tutored Joseph.

Ammon, one of the great missionaries talked about in the very plates Joseph translated with the help of God and angels, had a conversation with Lamoni that reveals important information on where angels live. Lamoni was a king, and a good one, but he did not know enough that would be valuable for his life through all eternity. Ammon asked the king if he believed there was a God or a Great Spirit. King Lamoni said he did. Then Ammon asked if the king understood that this almighty power was the creator of the world and all things that were in heaven and in the earth. King Lamoni replied to Ammon that he believed the creator made all the things which are in the earth; but, he added, "I do not know the heavens." Then Ammon taught Lamoni the wonderful truth,

"The heavens is a place where God dwells and all his holy angels." As Ammon continued this line of teaching, King Lamoni ultimately was converted.[28]

But there is still another aspect to the time frame of angels and their comings and goings between heaven and earth. God's dwelling place is a house of order. Laws have been irrevocably decreed in heaven before the foundations of this world, upon which all blessings are predicated and which impact all of God's creations.[29] He set the sun, the moon, and the stars in heaven to rise and set according to their governing laws; the sea tides and currents function according to their bounds. The Prophet Joseph Smith taught that all things move in perfect harmony in their sphere and order and are lights and wonders and signs to us.[30] This view is in harmony with scriptures but also with facts from the scientific world. Children learn this in school and adults witness it over and over again in the seasons of life.

The Prophet Joseph added a dimension of insight that is vital to our understanding of angel visits, angel time frames, and our own coming and going from heaven to earth and back—our own placement and time frame, if you will. He said, "It is a decree of the Lord that every tree, plant, and herb bearing seed should bring forth of its own kind, and cannot come forth after any other law or principle. Upon the same principle do I contend that baptism is a sign ordained of God, for the believer in Christ to take upon himself in order to enter into the kingdom of God, 'for except ye are born of water and of the Spirit ye cannot enter into the Kingdom of God,' said the Savior. It is a sign and a commandment which

God has set for man to enter into His Kingdom. Those who seek to enter in any other way will seek in vain; for God will not receive them, *neither will the angels acknowledge their works as accepted,* for they have not obeyed the ordinances, nor attended to the signs which God ordained for the salvation of man, to prepare him for, and give him a title to, a celestial glory."[31]

Understanding the time frame and reality of real angels also is helpful to attaining the correct LDS perspective about murder, suicide, abortion, pregnancy out of wedlock, and deathbed repentance. We abort the laws when we act as God in the matter of time frames for living and dying! We should solemnly consider these things. By the same token, we should keep ourselves well physically and spiritually so that we can serve God in good health while we are on earth. This is a matter that deserves our pondering regarding our faith, our behavior, and our entitlement to God's will for us.

The governing laws and commandments of all phases and elements of life were decreed because they work, they bring about the desired result, they are part of the creative bounds since before the foundations of this world.

When we delve into the mysteries of God, we find ourselves in the company of Moses on the Mount being tutored. Moses beheld every particle of the earth, discerning it by the Spirit of God. He beheld those who would eventually inhabit the earth in our day, and they were as numerous as the sands on the seas. Moses asked why these things are so, and "by what thou madest them?" Imagine the incredible experience for Moses to stand in the presence of God (and this while the children of Israel whom he was leading out of captivity were building their idol god—a golden calf, of all things!) to learn that, "For mine own purpose have I made these things. Here is wisdom and it remaineth in me."[32]

Valuable information on this subject is found in Doctrine and Covenants 130. A summary of this section follows:

Angels live on and on and on in different phases of being. So do we.

Angels reside in the presence of God, on a globe like a sea of glass and fire, where all things for their glory—past, present, future—are made known to them.

Angels' time (and God's time and man's time) is according to the planet on which they reside at any given time.

Angels do not minister to this earth unless they belong to it or have belonged to it or will belong to it.

Angels as messengers of Heavenly Father are chosen from among His offspring and are themselves pressing forward along the course of progress according to the time frame of their sphere.

Angels do not always reveal their names, or at least this fact is not always recorded. Through the power of the Holy Ghost a mortal may recognize an angel as an ancestor or a future earth descendant who comes on a specific mission.

Angels and the Holy Ghost must not be confused as to their respective assignment, calling, mission. Angels speak through the power of the Holy Ghost, who is a member of the Godhead.

The same sociality which we know here will exist in heaven only if coupled with eternal glory. We will see our

THE TRUTH ABOUT ANGELS

loved ones again, and they will be familiar to us! When the Savior shall appear we shall see Him as a person like whom we are trying to become.

The following is vital information to anyone wanting to learn the truth about angels:

"When a messenger comes saying he has a message from God, offer him your hand and request him to shake hands with you. If he be an angel he will do so, and you will feel his hand. If he be the spirit of a just man made perfect he will come in his glory; for that is the only way he can appear—Ask him to shake hands with you, but he will not move, because it is contrary to the order of heaven for a just man to deceive; but he will still deliver his message. If it be the devil as an angel of light, when you ask him to shake hands he will offer you his hand, and you will not feel anything; you may therefore detect him."[33]

Meanwhile, let us open our hearts so that we may be moved upon to act like angels ourselves while making a worthwhile contribution here on earth.

NOTES

1. 1 Nephi 7:9–10.
2. Joseph Smith—History 1:30–32, 43.
3. Doctrine and Covenants 20:6.
4. 1 Nephi 1:8–10.
5. Daniel 3:27, 28.

6. Zechariah 5:9.

7. See Doctrine and Covenants 77:4.

8. Acts 2:2.

9. See *History of the Church* 2:428.

10. *History of the Church* 3:392.

11. Doctrine and Covenants 132:37.

12. See Genesis 28:20–22.

13. Job 1:6.

14. Lavier Leon Depour, ed., *Dictionary of Biblical Theology* (New York City: Seabury Press, 1995), p. 377.

15. 1 Peter 3:22.

16. 3 Nephi 28:25.

17. See Hebrews 13:2.

18. Mormon 8:11.

19. Mosiah 27:14.

20. Doctrine and Covenants 29:42.

21. 2 Nephi 32:3.

22. See Doctrine and Covenants 128:21.

23. John 20:15.

24. Mosiah 3:3.

25. See Helaman 5:36–49.

26. Doctrine and Covenants 130:4.

27. Luke 1:19.

28. Alma 18:29–30; see verses 18–40.

29. See Doctrine and Covenants 130:20–21.

30. See Joseph Smith, *Teachings of the Prophet Joseph Smith*, comp. Joseph Fielding Smith (Salt Lake City: Deseret Book Co., 1976), p. 197.

31. Ibid.; emphasis added.

32. Moses 1:30–31.

33. Doctrine and Covenants 129:4–8.

Six

WHAT
DO ANGELS DO?

*S*hakespeare long has been quoted by mothers lulling their sons with, "Good night, sweet prince, and flights of angels sing thee to thy rest."[1] This line was appropriately used as the epitaph on the marker of the world-acclaimed star of *Hamlet* and other theater works, Sir Lawrence Olivier. Before the two great World Wars and the loss of real civility, scores of lullabies and love songs centered on sentimental messages of angels creeping around the rocking cradle or spreading flower petals around the marriage bed as symbols of joy. People *wanted* angels scattering blessings in such key moments of life. But they only knew a fraction of the truth about angels.

What angels do is often well disguised, but may it suffice to say that God is there for us and his angels stand by to do his bidding. We look to Alma for a strong statement of how angels help God by providing vital, sacred service.

At one point, Alma stretched forth his hands to a great multitude and cried out in a mighty, passionate voice: "Now is the time to repent, for the day of salvation draweth nigh; yea, and the voice of the Lord, *by the mouth of angels,* doth declare it unto all nations; . . . the joyful news [is] declared unto us by the mouth of angels, of his coming."[2] This was about eighty-two years before the birth of Christ. An important scripture often overlooked in our own days of doubt reminds us that it is "*by faith that angels appear* and minister unto men; wherefore, if these things have ceased wo be unto the children of men, for it is because of unbelief, and all is vain."[3]

However, it is wrenching to realize that for Alma's great wisdom and eloquent teaching on such an important subject as angels he was thrown in prison and smitten. Any who believed in Alma and Amulek's God were burned by fire![4]

The scriptures detail God's ongoing relationship with man. This interaction is accomplished through the power of the Holy Ghost and through angels—angels from heaven and often angels who are kindly people still living on earth and who are heaven's helpers, too. The examples are numerous, beautiful, comforting, marvelous, and true! But they must not be spoken of lightly. The spiritually prepared soul values those great and memorable moments when the speaker and listener understand one another, both being edified and rejoicing together. Scriptural counsel comes from heaven and is holy and sacred and should be spoken of with care—"by constraint of the Spirit."[5] (Remember that to *constrain* is not to restrain but to compel! The Spirit must almost force us to speak of such sacred events.) The witness of God's caring about us actually comes from heaven itself for he said, "I Jesus have sent mine angel to testify unto you these things."[6]

There are specific instances when God has said he would send his angels. One dramatic statement describes the tribulation of the last days before Christ comes again. It speaks of the tribes of the earth mourning until "the Son of Man shall come, and he shall send his angels before him with the great sound of a trumpet, and they shall gather together the remainder of his elect from the four winds, from one end of heaven to the other." This exciting information precedes the parable of the fig tree and is implicit with the warning for all to be ready for that great day.[7]

The Lord has kept his word to send his angels before people on specific errands of helpfulness. In situations that range from the teaching of the gospel to Adam and his seed, to Abraham's dispatching his servant to claim a wife for Isaac, to the finding of the promised land in two dispensations of time, to releasing God's prophets from captivity, angels have been sent by God to earth.[8] Clearly angels are heavenly messengers sent forth to minister to inhabitants of earth. Even if we have not personally been visited by angels, we still are beneficiaries.

Angels are dispensers and administrators of divine beneficence to us; they regard our safety, undertake our defense, direct our ways, and exercise a constant solicitude.[9] Angels minister to God's children and perform needful things relative to his work.[10] Angels teach the doctrines of salvation.[11] Angels save God's children in perilous circumstances.[12] They guide people in the performance of his work[13] and gather his elect in the last days.[14] Angels announced the resurrection of Christ.[15] Moroni 7:29–31 states: "Have miracles ceased? Behold I say unto you, Nay; neither have angels ceased to minister unto the children of men. For behold, they are subject unto him, to minister according to the word of his command, showing themselves unto them of strong faith and a firm mind in every form of godliness. And the office of their ministry is to call men unto repentance, and to fulfil and to do the work of the covenants of the Father, which he hath made unto the children of men, to prepare the way among the children of men, by declaring the word of Christ unto the chosen vessels of the Lord, that they may bear testimony of him."

Elder Marion D. Hanks said, "There are no casual angels who minister specifically to us. They are ancestors or loved ones who have gone on to heaven or they are spirits of posterity yet to come."[16] Angels can be those who have lived on earth and died, returning to heaven, and then being sent back to earth briefly for some specific reason. They love and care for us yet. There are countless instances of appearances of angels who have been recognized as someone who had returned to earth to perform some worthy act.

President Joseph F. Smith surely had the view of life's continuum from premortal life through earth life to exaltation. He often linked angels with mortals in an understandable way. He said, "Surely those who have passed beyond can see more clearly through the veil back here to us than it's possible for us to see to them from our sphere of action. I believe we move and have our being in the presence of heavenly messengers and of heavenly beings. We are not separate from them. . . . We are closely related to our kindred, to our ancestors, to our friends and associates and co-laborers who have preceded us into the spirit world. We cannot forget them; we do not cease to love them; we always hold them in our hearts: . . . They know us better than we know them. . . . They have advanced and we are advancing."[17]

Angels are neither myth nor metaphor, although mortals may choose to view or depict them this way. From lullabies to epitaphs, wrestling to ordaining, escorting hapless spirits to Satan's murky place or tenderly ushering the worthy into celestial spheres, what angels do varies with their heavenly call to duty and their personal preparation to perform.

NOTES

1. William Shakespeare, *Hamlet,* Act 5, scene 2.
2. Alma 13:21–22, 25; emphasis added.
3. Moroni 7:37; emphasis added.
4. See Alma 14:8.
5. Doctrine and Covenants 63:64.
6. Revelation 22:16.
7. Joseph Smith—Matthew 1:37.
8. See Doctrine and Covenants 29:42; Genesis 24:7; Exodus

23:20; Doctrine and Covenants 103:19–20.

    9. See John Calvin, *Institutes of the Christian Religion* (Grand Rapids, Mich.: Eerdmans, 1986).

    10. See Luke 1:11–38.

    11. See Mosiah 3.

    12. See Helaman 5.

    13. See Doctrine and Covenants 103:19–20.

    14. See Matthew 24:31.

    15. See Luke 24:1–7; Matthew 28:1–6.

    16. Funeral of Christine Jacobsen Cannon, January 1975.

    17. Joseph F. Smith, in Conference Report, April 1916, p. 3.

Seven

THE ANGEL SAID, "FEAR NOT!"

*A*lmost two thousand years ago an amazing miracle happened in the midst of a rather sophisticated setting for its day. Jerusalem was a city of history, culture, commerce, social tradition, and intricate relationships between nations and races. Among the thousands were those few who had eyes to see and ears to hear a singular event that would change life for everyone always. Humble shepherds, keeping watch over their flocks of sheep and lambs in a grazing field somewhere between Bethlehem and the sacred city of Jerusalem, saw angels and heard good tidings of great joy.

Maybe you have been to Shepherds' Fields of an evening to sit on a rock and watch the shepherds and the sheep in a pastoral scene almost unchanged from two thousand years ago and to meditate on the sweet and silent night of long ago when Christ was born. Those early shepherds were "sore afraid" because in the quiet of their night an angel of the Lord appeared to them and the glory of the Lord shone round about them. To the shepherds the angel said, "Fear not: for, behold, I bring you good tidings of great joy, which shall be to all people. For unto you is born this day in the city of David a Saviour, which is Christ the Lord. And this shall be a sign unto you; Ye shall find the babe wrapped in swaddling clothes, lying in a manger."[1] And it was so.

That message of the angel revealed several important items of information:

- "fear not": no need to feel anxiety because this angel brings news from God; and God is comfort and peace, not fear.
- "tidings of great joy": here is a message like nothing ever heard before, one to pierce the soul with its significance and its promise of happiness.
- "all people": everybody who ever lived or will yet live will be affected by this announcement.
- "born this day . . . a savior": fulfilling an ancient prophecy with portentous future impact.
- "a sign unto you": make no mistake, there is only a stable and swaddling clothes involved here, not a palace for a king with guards to watch—but angels and a manger for a sign.

The heralding angel was joined by a multitude of the heavenly host. Among that host might have been angels who were prophets of old and who had foretold this event; perhaps spirits unborn yet who would become God's special servants in a later day; even seers through the unfolding ages. There was much praising of God in the highest and a prediction of ultimate peace in the hearts of mankind on earth—particularly those hearts in tune with God and the whole remarkable plan of life as prepared by him for his creations.

Incredible! Wonderful! So sweet a thing that we melt inside at the thought! Christians renew their gratitude as they celebrate this event each year with a rehearsal of the birth of Jesus the Christ, the Son of God, the awaited Messiah, the Firstborn of the Father and his Only Begotten in the flesh. Since then, artisans, musicians, and writers, as well as school children, have built the wonder of a worldwide Christmas celebration out of shepherds, a stable, an innocent babe, and angels—angels, angels, and more angels, so acceptable in early times. The Christmas of worship and praise is replete with references to angels. After all, they brought the news and marked the miracle; their presence helped validate Jesus as the Son of God.

Christina Rossetti, a pre-Raphaelite associate, modeled for her artist brother, Dante Gabriel, and others of the group in the mid-1800s who were into angelology. Christina was a distinguished poet as well and wrote these tender lines:

> Angels and archangels may have gathered there,
> Cherubim and seraphim thronged the air;
> But his mother only, in her maiden bliss,
> Worshipped the Beloved with a kiss.

The restored gospel has added a dimension to the biblical first Christmas. We know that some of the plain and precious truths have been omitted from the Bible, as if by subtle design by Satan to keep the fulness of understanding from people.[2] Robert Matthews, credible Church scholar and teacher, has suggested that the Bible may tell *what* has happened in religious history, but latter-day revelation tells *why*. It is fortunate that the people in Jerusalem were not the only ones on earth to know about the birth of a Savior for mankind. At the time that angels announced the birth of baby Jesus in Bethlehem, angels also appeared in ancient America. On that holy night, there were great signs given that fulfilled the prophecies that Christ was born: "Thus in this year the scriptures began to be fulfilled."[3]

Not every one in those communities understood what was happening, however. Only those who had listened to the prophets were caught up in the sureness of the miracle of angels in their midst heralding Christ. When people do not listen, they do not hear, and their foolish lack of understanding and their mistaken notions soon become apparent. In that day, for example, in Zarahemla, when prophets recognized signs prophesying Jesus' birth, scoffers proclaimed that it was not reasonable for a being such as the Son of God the Father of heaven and of earth to come and dwell among plain people! If so, they reasoned: "Why will he not show himself unto us as well as unto them who shall be at Jerusalem? Yea, why will he not show himself in this land as well as in the land of Jerusalem?"[4] Of course, we know that he did visit those Nephite people just thirty-three years later. This thrilling, telling truth is recorded in the Book of Mormon.[5]

Even before the angels heralded the good news of the birth of Jesus, an angel had visited Mary instructing her to fear not! Then he announced, "Hail thou that are highly favored, the Lord is with thee: blessed art thou among women."[6] Mary was chosen by God for a unique destiny, and she learned this stunning news from a supernatural being. This same angel, Gabriel, also appeared to Joseph and said, "Joseph . . . fear not to take unto thee Mary thy wife: for that which is conceived in her is of the Holy Ghost. And she shall bring forth a son, and thou shalt call his name JESUS: for he shall save his people from their sins."[7]

After Jesus' birth, Joseph again was visited by an angel— one might call him a guardian angel because he came to warn Joseph to take Mary and the child into Egypt as a protection against the wicked King Herod. When Herod died, an angel came again to Joseph and told him to leave Egypt and go back to the land of Israel.[8] As a practical matter to avoid any problems with Herod's son Archelaus, Joseph took the blessed child and its mother to dwell in Nazareth. This, not so incidentally, fulfilled what was spoken by early prophets that the son of God would be called a Nazarene.[9] Angels later supported Jesus in the trials of preparation for his earthly ministry.[10]

Later in life angels again ministered to Jesus. During the transfiguration of Jesus witnessed by his disciples Peter and James, "his raiment became shining, exceeding white as snow; so as no fuller on earth can white them. And there appeared unto them Elias with Moses: and they were talking with Jesus."[11]

It is very significant to remember that at the end of Christ's earthly mission—after all the miracles, including his calming of the storm over Galilee—Christ's suffering in Gethsemane was so great that he cried out to God to let the cup or the trial ahead pass from him. But as the "great drops of blood [fell] to the ground" *an angel* from heaven appeared to him and *strengthened* him.[12] To *strengthen* means to invigorate or increase mental, physical, or moral capacity or the will and power to perform or work.

Angels were not on hand, however, to *prevent* Christ's death on the cross. Without Christ's willingness to suffer it through and "give up the ghost,"[13] his resurrection would not have been accomplished. One of the dramatic details of this event involved Peter, who drew his sword and smote off the ear of one of the men who had come to take Christ captive. Christ, you recall, told Peter to put up his sword, adding, "Thinkest thou that I cannot now pray to my Father, and he shall presently give me more than twelve legions of angels?"[14] Christ knew that this was not the time for such help.

Most Christians are well versed in these things, but in studying the work and lineage, if you will, of the empowerment of angels, we emphasize again the significant part that angels played throughout the entire life and mission of the Savior. God the Creator can send angelic messengers to give warning and instruction according to his purposes.

After the Crucifixion, angels appeared at the Lord's sepulchre. While Mary Magdalene and Mary the mother of

James kept watch by the tomb, as was the custom of the day, "The angel of the Lord descended from heaven, and came and rolled back the stone from the door, and sat upon it."[15] In Mark's version of this angelic appearance, the two Marys were surprised to find the stone door to the sepulchre rolled back. As they entered they saw a "young man sitting on the right side, clothed in a long white garment; and they were affrighted. And he saith unto them, Be not affrighted: [fear not!] Ye seek Jesus of Nazareth, which was crucified; he is risen; he is not here: behold the place where they laid him."[16]

The greatest hope of mankind is life after death. It was an angel of the Lord who uttered the beautiful but shocking words of great joy to fear not because he who had been crucified was risen!

Following the resurrection, a cloud received Christ and he was taken out of their sight. Two men stood by in white apparel and said, "Ye men of Galilee, why stand ye gazing up into heaven? this same Jesus, which is taken up from you into heaven, shall so come in like manner as ye have seen him go into heaven."[17]

Angels are connected with the Savior in another important way yet to unfold. The details of Christ's coming to usher in the millennium includes the *innumerable company of angels.* Some people in our day have had the promise given in a patriarchal blessing that they would be present at Christ's second coming. Some have already passed forward to eternal life—they are dead already! Yet still their promise from God in a patriarchal blessing can be accomplished from their spirit state beyond the grave.

One of the more descriptive scriptural offerings on the Second Coming is found in the second epistle of Paul the Apostle to the Thessalonians. Paul offers comfort by explaining to those who have lost loved ones through death, for example, that there will be retribution for the ungodly, and for the righteous there will be recompense for tribulation. When the Lord comes again he shall be revealed from heaven with his mighty angels in flaming fire. He will come and be glorified in his Saints.[18]

Certain signs will accompany the Lord Jesus when he comes to earth to reign in righteousness. One example appropriate to our discussion on angels is explained by Jesus himself. He promised that the tribes of the earth who are righteous shall see the clouds of heaven ushering the Son of God in power and great glory. And he will send angels with a great sound of a trumpet, gathering together from one end of heaven to the other.[19]

We know from holy revelation that the humble birth of Christ and the agony of his death will be reversed when he comes again. He will come in power and great glory with the hosts of heaven attending, and "the glory of the Lord shall be revealed, and all flesh shall see it together."[20]

In all humility, we mention the glorious promise that the participants in the work of the restoration of the fulness of the gospel truth know. "When the Savior shall appear we shall see him as he is. We shall see that he is a man like ourselves [only perfected]. And that same sociality which exists among us here will exist among us there, only it will be coupled with eternal glory, which glory we do not now enjoy."[21] Such is our blessing, based upon our keeping His law.[22] Such is the orderliness of God's work and ways. He who made his angels' spirits will come again, accompanied by ten thousands of them. "The chariots of God are twenty thousand, even thousands of angels."[23]

So fear not!

NOTES

1. Luke 2:10–12.
2. See 1 Nephi 13:26–28.
3. Helaman 16:14.
4. Helaman 16:18–19.
5. See 3 Nephi 11:1–10.
6. Luke 1:28.
7. Matthew 1:20–21.
8. See Matthew 2:13, 19–21.
9. See Matthew 2:23.
10. See Matthew 4:1–11.
11. Mark 9:3–4.
12. Luke 22:43–44.
13. See Mark 15:37.
14. Matthew 26:51–53; see also John 18:10.
15. Matthew 28:2.
16. Mark 16:5–6.
17. Acts 1:11.
18. See 2 Thessalonians 1:10.

19. See Matthew 24:31.
20. Isaiah 40:5.
21. Doctrine and Covenants 130:1–2.
22. See Doctrine and Covenants 130:20–21.
23. Psalm 68:17.

Eight

ANGELS AND TEMPLES OF GOD

*A*ngels and temples are constants on the long path of life. Heavenly Father has designated temples for our spiritual learning; and because of the significant, sacred nature of temples, inevitably angels have been present. Nephi was a strong and devout leader who one day waxed bold in prayer before God; that night "angels came down and ministered" to him.[1] He apparently received instruction about how to build a temple because, as he said, "I did construct it after the manner of the temple of Solomon save it were not built of so many precious things; for they were not to be found upon the land."[2]

Jacob, younger brother of Nephi, was a later prophet privileged to be directed by God through his ministering angels. The record says, "I, Jacob, gave unto [the people] these words as I taught them in the temple, having first obtained mine errand from the Lord."[3] Jacob went on to explain that he and his brother Joseph had been consecrated priests and teachers of their people, and subsequently gave powerful counsel on chastity. King Benjamin's oft-quoted last sermon was delivered to his people who had gathered in and about the temple. He emphasized that the great truths he shared were sent from God by an angel, who said unto him, "Awake, and hear the words which I shall tell thee; for behold, I am come to declare unto you the glad tidings of great joy. For the Lord hath heard thy prayers; . . . thou mayest declare unto thy people, that they may also be filled with joy."[4]

A significant example of spiritual manifestations in connection with temples was the gathering at the temple in the land Bountiful of the righteous who had survived the destruction on the earth when Christ was crucified. The people marveled at the changes that had occurred in their own community. They talked of the signs of Christ's death. While they thus were speaking, they heard a voice from heaven. It was God the Father introducing his Son, and they saw him descending out of heaven! Clad in a white robe was Jesus the Christ! Jesus introduced himself and at once began teaching the people the fulness of his gospel.[5]

Generations later, the first temple of The Church of Jesus Christ of Latter-day Saints was dedicated in Kirtland, Ohio, in 1836. The plans for this temple were revealed in exact detail by an angel to Joseph Smith. During the dedication ceremonies, this temple was full of angels and Church members alike. Many people saw angels or recognized that they were there. A marvelous heavenly manifestation to the whole congregation happened during Brother George A. Smith's prophesying. Suddenly "a noise was heard like the sound of a rushing mighty wind, which filled the Temple, and all the congregation simultaneously arose, being moved upon by an invisible power." People then saw the angels, and the temple itself was surrounded with a pillar of fire. It was at once marvelous and astonishing.[6]

Joseph Smith—repeatedly visited, tutored, and ministered to by angels—ended his dedicatory prayer of the Kirtland Temple with these words: "Help us by the power of thy Spirit, that we may mingle our voices with those *bright, shining seraphs* around thy throne, with acclamations of praise, singing Hosanna to God and the Lamb!"[7]

Today Latter-day Saints recognize the importance of angels by topping the center spire of their temples with a statue of the angel Moroni, who holds with one hand a trumpet symbolizing the announcement of the restored gospel. In the other hand he holds a replica of the gold plates from which the Book of Mormon was translated.

Besides a colorful career as a great leader and warrior, Moroni also had become the archivist of all the records of his Nephite ancestors which his own father, the prophet Mormon, had abridged. Just before he died and buried the plates containing the records, Moroni ended this record with these significant words of his own: "If it be wisdom in God that ye should read [these things], that ye would remember how merciful the Lord hath been unto the children of men, from the creation of Adam even down until the time that ye shall receive these things, and ponder it in your hearts. And when ye shall receive these things, I would exhort you that ye would ask God, the Eternal Father, in the name of Christ, if these things are not true; and if ye shall ask with a sincere heart, with real intent, having faith in Christ, he will manifest the truth of it unto you, by the power of the Holy Ghost. And by the power of the Holy Ghost ye may know the truth of all things."[8]

On the Hill Cumorah near Palmyra, New York, where Moroni gave Joseph Smith the gold plates, is the ten-foot bronze figure of Moroni, mounted on a twenty-five foot shaft of white granite. He points toward heaven with his right hand and holds a replica of the plates with the left. Created by Norwegian sculpture Torlief S. Knaphus, the monument was dedicated by Church President Heber J. Grant on 21 July 1935.[9]

The *Encyclopedia of Mormonism* states, "Moroni was the last in a line of prophet-leaders in the Western Hemisphere whose history is recorded in the Book of Mormon. Latter-day Saints believe John the Revelator foretold Moroni's angelic ministry: 'And I saw another angel fly in the midst of heaven, having the everlasting gospel to preach unto them that dwell on the earth, and to every nation, and kindred, and tongue, and people' (Revelation 14:6)."[10]

Today the angel Moroni is one of the most widely recognized LDS symbols or artistic images. Artist renderings of this heavenly messenger vary. I had a conversation with a clerk in a store that sells souvenirs and materials about the Church. I asked for pictures of the various sculptures of the angel Moroni used in various temples. He insisted that all of the angels on all the temples were exactly alike. I disagreed with him because I knew otherwise. He said, "It's Moroni, isn't it—that angel? So what's to be different?" He was insistent, absolutely certain of his opinion, and he also was young and inexperienced.

It may be an easy mistake to believe that because these angels touching the worldwide skies above scattered LDS temples all represent Moroni, they are exactly alike. Part of the wonder of researching angels for this manuscript has been to learn otherwise. They are not alike. As an art form, they have been rendered by several different sculptors, just as there are countless expressions by painters of the Holy Family. Each work reflects the artist's own perspective. In the Museum of Church History and Art in Salt Lake City, Utah, there are several different models of the heralding angel Moroni. These personal artistic interpretations do not lessen the truths that Moroni lived as a man—a warrior, a servant of the Lord, a recordkeeper, a craftsman of metal plates upon which sacred engravings were etched permanently and which were crafted to last for eons of time.

Moroni was a person and an angel unique from, say, Moses as a person or an angel. Each angel looks like himself— enhanced and glorified as angels, to be sure, but the essence of each individual is unique and eternal. God's spirit children (though housed at some point in mortal bodies) are who we are and will always be.

Over 150 years ago on the banks of the Mississippi River, the new Nauvoo Temple spire featured a horizontal angel. This angel wore billowing, floating robes and a *halo hat* and carried the heralding trump. Designed in the charming but quaint mode of woodcut weather vanes of the day, this angel is clearly visible in William Week's early designs of the Nauvoo Temple. The Nauvoo Temple was built at great sacrifice by the Saints, but it was destroyed by arsonist enemies of the Church before the Saints began the trek across the plains west to the Great Salt Lake Valley.

In earliest times of the Church, certain symbols of the temple covenants were used as part of the design on the mounting rod itself which secured the angel Moroni to a spire. This practice later was abandoned.

Early architectural drawings of the Salt Lake Temple also first showed plans for the horizontal, weather vane type of angel Moroni. However, before the temple was completed, the plan changed. Moroni became an upright figure of sturdy dignity with a longer trumpet to herald the incredibly good news of the gospel fully revealed and institutionalized in this latter dispensation of time. Several designers and sculptors over the years have been responsible for various symbolic representations of Moroni in statue form. The one that pierces the sky from the highest eastern spire of the Salt Lake Temple was sculpted by Cyrus E. Dallin, a sculptor of international note who was born in Springville, Utah. Dallin was not a member of the LDS Church at the time and questioned whether he could sculpt an angel when he had never seen one!

"The closest thing to an angel I've ever seen is my mother," Dallin is credited with saying. This beloved figure of Moroni was designed in the classic Roman style with a hairstyle reminiscent of a winner's laurel wreath headpiece.

The figure's robes are flowing and rather feminine, as are the features and hands—perhaps after Dallin's mother! Later angel Moroni statues rectified this and the models were deliberately made more masculine with narrow, straight lines in the robes and a strong, clenched grip in the left hand, for example. This Salt Lake Temple angel by Cyrus Dallin is clearly and dramatically visible at close range from the special view window in the Museum of Church History and Art west of the temple and from the roof garden at the Joseph Smith Memorial Building east of Temple Square. Cyrus Dallin also was the sculptor of the Brigham Young monument in the center of Main Street, also just east of Temple Square.

Dr. Avard Tennyson Fairbanks (1897–1987) won a Church competition for a heroic-size (twice the size of life) statue of the angel Moroni. He represents the Nephite prophet Moroni as a resurrected being with the gold plates in one hand, with his other hand holding to his lips the heralding trumpet. This statue was sculpted in clay, bronzed, and then covered with many layers of gold leaf. The Fairbanks model tops temples in Washington, D.C.; Mexico City; Jordan River in south Salt Lake City, Utah; and Seattle, Washington.

The angel Moroni statues currently are constructed to meet building requirements in many countries and are made from fiberglass forms that are then covered in gold leaf. The design is the result of a prayerful team effort of sculptor Karl Quilter and manufacturer LaVar Wallgren of 3 D Art, Inc., of Kearns, Utah. This Moroni model was deliberately designed to reveal muscular strength and masculine features. The model was first sculpted in clay, sprayed with tinted gel-coat, and then wrapped by hand with wet sheets of fiberglass to make a mold. The process is repeated inside the mold, and the new statue is allowed to set up before it is covered with many layers of gold leaf and polished. It comes in two sizes to suit the requirements of each particular temple. Measured from heel to head, this angel Moroni statue is either seven feet or twelve feet high. There are twenty-seven temples so far that bear the fiberglass statue in gold leaf.

There are many anecdotes about temples and angels—some inevitably apocryphal—that circulate among the Saints across the world. However, the following is a true story from my own experience, which also is recorded in personal records of others involved. It is about the angel that tops the lovely Los Angeles Temple.

The construction of the Los Angeles Temple in the early 1950s was momentous. People were excited about the project because it marked a new era of expansion for the Church. The local Church members in that area famous for flare and talent had strong opinions about its appearance. The angel itself was a new design. During that time I had business to transact in the Buehner Company plant in Murray, Utah. I was thrilled to learn that this company was preparing the angel for the new Los Angeles Temple spire. Paul Buehner escorted me into a far end of the facility to see this new angel Moroni. The figure was ready for its plaster mold, which would then be crated and shipped to the Roman Bronze foundry in New York, where it would be cast in aluminum and covered with gold leaf. Now there it was in gray clay, flat on its back, stretched to heroic size, impressive. It was indeed worthy as an art piece to top the new temple—a building that was creating a great stir among local residents. This angel would be seen for miles by hundreds of thousands who passed by on the freeways of Southern California.

Mr. Buehner directed me to the enormous left foot of the angel where the initials "M. C." had been deeply etched in the big toenail! Mr. Buehner stroked it almost reverently and certainly with tenderness. He explained that Elder Matthew Cowley, one of the Twelve Apostles at that time and beloved as a spiritual giant with a great sense of occasion as well as humor, had come to inspect the angel sculpture while the clay was still damp. Because Matthew Cowley had lived in California for many years before he became an Apostle, the Los Angeles Temple was a special, personal project. Therefore, this angel inspection was significant for Elder Cowley. Paul Buehner described the joy and emotion of Elder Cowley as he studied the statue. I could understand that feeling as I listened to this story while I examined the impressive angel sculpture. Elder Cowley was so excited about the angel that on an incredible impulse he decided to leave his own loving stamp of approval—he carefully carved his initials "M. C." on the big toenail of the angel's huge left foot. The Buehner Company decided to leave in the etching.

The day came when the angel was readied and hoisted into position on the center spire of the Los Angeles Temple. At the dedication of the temple itself, Elder and Sister Cowley were among the General Authorities and their wives invited to participate in the ceremonies. A twist of irony in the story is that Elder Cowley went to bed that night after the events, thrilled with the realization of his dream, and died in his sleep. He was fifty-seven years old.

Nearly twenty years later I was in Washington, D.C., on assignment when that elegant temple was being built near the busy beltway of the nation's capital. The massive angel Moroni was to be hoisted by an enormous crane high up to its place on the center spire. The day before the ceremonies, our group visited the temple site while the last of the crating around the huge statue was being removed. I thought of Elder Cowley and his tender affection for the Los Angeles angel Moroni. Though I didn't scratch my initials, I simply could not resist firmly rubbing my thumb over the gold big toe nail of the giant-size left foot of that sculpture of angel Moroni.

The next day people gathered for the exciting moment when the statue would be hoisted through the air skyward to its high place on the center spire. The enormous crane was in place, the angel properly secured, and the signal was given. But as the angel statue was partway up the flight to the top spire, the long crane crumpled under its weight. A gasp erupted from the crowd watching the angel dangle in the bent steel. The mounting had to be postponed for some days until new arrangements could be made.

Nonetheless, soon the angel Moroni statue found its position of honor on the top spire. The Washington Temple was completed and the ground about it landscaped. Washington, D.C., is the embassy capital of the world, and an impressive number of dignitaries, royalty, service heroes, politicians, and their families joined in the public open house to view the building inside and out before its dedication. A joyful spirit was exceedingly high during the 1974 dedication ceremonies of that landmark temple.

In the group coming from Church headquarters for the occasion was Sister Freda Joan Lee, widow of President Harold B. Lee, who had been such a force behind the building of this new temple east of the Mississippi. President Lee had passed away unexpectedly almost a year before the dedication of the Washington Temple. At the conclusion of the ceremonies President Hugh B. Brown, who had served as a counselor to President Lee in the First Presidency, greeted Sister Lee affectionately, saying he had just had a long and satisfying visit "with your Harold!" A true believer in angels, in life after death, and in the power of and command of God (as well as the veracity of President Brown), Sister Lee was truly comforted, though admittedly a bit jealous!

Neither temples nor angels are an endangered species in The Church of Jesus Christ of Latter-day Saints. Temples dot the face of the earth in increasing numbers. Many have a statue of the angel Moroni on top, and all have the precious spiritual ministering of the Lord Jesus Christ's work inside.

NOTES

1. 2 Nephi 4:24.
2. 2 Nephi 5:16.

3. Jacob 1:17; see also verses 18–19.

4. Mosiah 3:3–4.

5. See 3 Nephi 11.

6. Bruce R. McConkie, *Mormon Doctrine,* 2nd ed. (Salt Lake City: Bookcraft, 1960), p. 181.

7. Doctrine and Covenants 109:79.

8. Moroni 10:3–5.

9. See *Encyclopedia of Mormonism,* s.v. "Angel Moroni Statue."

10. Ibid.

Nine

How Truth
Became Error

The Sistine Chapel in Rome—star of the Vatican, masterpiece of Michelangelo, and for centuries the favorite site of traveling pilgrims and tourists thronging the sacred rotunda—has been restored, only recently, to its original grandeur. It now is a classic example of how truth becomes error.

Startling discoveries were made as the cleaning progressed on the magnificent creation scenes painted on the dome. Incredibly, artists had *painted over* and *added to* Michelangelo's original painting. According to archivists and historians, this likely was done over the generations to reflect the changing philosophies of artists and clergy. Those in charge of the restoration were shocked and argued the merits of protecting the additions to the masterpiece or restoring the original work itself by cleaning away later additions by other artists. Blessedly, it was determined to protect Michelangelo's original work.

It is my understanding that all but thirteen angels had their wings removed. In truth, Michelangelo's angels originally had been painted without wings! Notable, too, is the fact that the filmy, billowing banner floating over the low portion of the Savior's body had been added long after Michelangelo's time. It was decided to remove this "modesty" covering to reveal the intent of the original work, which was to represent that mankind had indeed been created in the image of God!

For centuries the Sistine Chapel work has fostered and underscored manmade beliefs of later periods to depict winged angels and a genderless God. Innocent efforts to explain angels flying from heaven resulted in artistic license that included attaching wings on human bodies to designate who was angel and who was man; in the same sense, the symbolic halo or circle of light about heavenly beings quickly became a design for a kind of headpiece in the hands of artists and clergy robing themselves to achieve respect.

Thus truth had become error.

It is significant that an angel revealed the details of how truth became error. In one comparatively short section of the Book of Mormon, an "angel of the Lord" explained to Nephi how the Bible had proceeded forth from the mouth of a Jew and remained in its fulness of the gospel of the Lord until it went in "purity unto the Gentiles." Then a "great and abominable church" was formed, and to gain power and "blind the eyes and harden the hearts" of people, they took away from the "gospel of the Lamb many parts which are plain and most precious" including many covenants. This perverted the "right ways of the Lord." Then the angel said to Nephi, "Wherefore, thou seest that after the book hath gone forth through the hands of the great and abominable church, that there are many plain and precious things taken away from the book, which is the book of the Lamb of God." Because this great loss of truth occurred and spread among people in all the lands, "an exceedingly great many do stumble, yea, insomuch that Satan hath great power over them."[1]

There also has been a thrilling restoration of the plain and precious things necessary for understanding the purpose of life and the salvation of mankind. To learn more about angels and Heavenly Father's family, a person must understand this. Sources must be dependable! Therefore, our most important sources for sharing the truth about real angels are the standard works of The Church of Jesus Christ of Latter-day Saints and the revelations from God to his prophets.

In every age and culture, people have used their own language, idiom, syntax, experiences, and personal frame of reference in expressing ideas—including such spiritual ideas as angels and God's use of them. It is important to remember that views on angels do not belong only to Christians. All of God's children since the beginning have had truth only as they were ready to receive it line upon line and preserve it in righteousness. The history of mankind speaks for itself about how error has crept in. This is why the restoration of gospel truth was necessary. It is why people today should seek truth in matters of God. Angels are of God, not of cultists, publicists, or craftsmen!

With regard to the translating and transmitting early Christian records for the New Testament, Dummelow's *Bible Commentary* (first copyrighted in 1908, a period of time which presented a more traditional biblical perspective) admits this intriguing information: "Nearly four thousand Greek manuscripts of the New Testament are known to exist. As a result, the variety of readings is considerable. But while we can see how intricate and difficult is the task of the New Testament scholars, we must remember, on the one hand, that the vast majority of the differences are unimportant; and, on the other hand, that where they are important we have in the providence of God such range of materials as no age has ever possessed for learning the truth. We can still search the scriptures in perfect confidence that they will testify of Christ, and that their testimony is true."[2]

Believers always have been taunted by skeptics. It is part of Satan's system for destroying Christ's work on earth. Joan of Arc's claim to hear heavenly voices and receive instruction through an ever-brightening light brought her ridicule. Her vision included angels led by Michael, which compelled her to certain acts of courage during the Crusades. Those who followed her believed her because of their own innate spiritual *in-tune-ness*. But saving France did not save Joan. The doubters reasoned that they never had seen an angel, a vision, or heard a heavenly voice, so how possibly could this village maiden have entertained a heavenly messenger?

It was 1431 when Joan was led captive to the cemetery in

Rouen, surprised and alarmed at the crowd that had gathered to rage and shout for her death. Joan was burned at the stake for heresy and sorcery. Generations later she was spoken of as an angel. In 1920, Pope Benedict XV canonized her by declaring her a saint. Churches were named after her. She knew that God knew that she had had a vision, and she could not deny this even to save her own life.

Joseph Smith was killed because he would not, could not, deny that he had seen God and been ministered to by angels. His mission in life was a calling from God to restore "plain and precious truths."

Often people lose faith because they do not know enough or what they know is falsely given. The truth about angels, God, principles of righteousness, exactness of God's laws, and continuing revelation had been forgotten or distorted over the centuries leading up to Joseph Smith's day, hindering full faith and belief! There are many reasons why this has happened.

For example, since the beginning, little was recorded on the subject of God, and translations have been imperfect. What was recorded and translated in early days was done in the context of the times and idiom of the day. Word usage has changed over the generations. For example, the King James Version of the Bible refers to a church leader or bishop in Ephesus as an *angel*, but the Joseph Smith Translation corrects this to *servant*, which is more understandable today.[3] Limited education and technology, incomplete secondhand telling of the tale, information massaged through distorted details supplied by personal fancy and interpretation.

Access to truth for the ordinary citizen was manipulated by clergy for personal power and gain. Knowledge of angels (and other religious traditions) was shallow among ordinary people. Such information was impeded for centuries by scant availability of teachers and texts among a tribal populace scattered over the land by agricultural pursuits. Religious doctrine suffered through the stages of apostasy—a silent heaven, near-darkness among a skeptical, scattered people. Also, some sacred traditions were altered through a shattered church hierarchy's controlling web and by contesting political factions. Self-styled religious practices were introduced to suit convenience—for example, baptism by immersion was replaced with sprinkling.

The evil or self-serving designs of people functioning without the Spirit of God added to confusion with only partial truths then passed from generation to generation. Doctrinal error followed quickly the crucifixion of Jesus and the subsequent deaths of Christ's disciples. Records became scattered. Attitudes of greed, hypocrisy, skepticism, and apostasy flourished.

Even today with truth restored, literacy high, temples dotting the world, and technology abounding for all kinds of information retrieval, there still are people who have not availed themselves of important information supplied through the Restoration—including the truth about angels. They are bereft of immensely beneficial knowledge. Knowledge of truth fosters belief. Belief supports experience, which strengthens faith. With faith all things are possible—the Red Sea was parted by the faith of the children of Israel. Mary became the mother of the Savior. Joseph Smith translated the unknown language on the record plates of ancient immigrants to the American continents. In another day the walls of Jericho tumbled. In modern times, crop-destroying crickets were devoured by the sudden miracle of seagulls. It is by faith that angels appear, and if God has withheld his power in this regard, "Wo be unto the children of men, for it is because of unbelief, and all is vain."[4]

Years ago Thoreau suggested, "People talk about Bible miracles because there is no miracle in their lives. Cease to gnaw that crust. There is ripe fruit over your head."

Scriptures studied with a specific purpose in mind, like finding out about angels, brings a wonderful, comforting witness. You'll see! You who understand the way God works, the channels he has established for us from our hearts to heaven, and the orderliness and perfection with which sacred things occur—you will find the study of angels of God absolutely confirming. There is a way to strengthen your own testimony about these things! The promise found in the last chapter of the book of Mormon includes how to know the truth about angels. Moroni—before he himself became an angel in the special service of God—engraved these following lines on the metal plates of his own making so that people who followed after him could know what he knew to be true. He exhorted people to read the gospel truths and ponder them in their hearts. Then he said, "And when ye shall receive these things, I would exhort you that ye would ask God, the Eternal Father, in the name of Christ, if these things are not true; and if ye shall ask with a sincere heart, with real intent, having faith in Christ, he will manifest the truth of it unto you, by the power of the Holy Ghost."[5]

Blessedly, by the power of the Holy Ghost you may know the truth of all things. You will be filled with pure Spirit to the extent that your heart will swell and your mind will be quickened, and you will be privileged to feel the unimpeachable witness of the truth about angels and other kinds of heavenly manifestations from God.

In addition to Moroni's inspired promise to all mankind, we emphasize here that all who have covenanted before God, angels, and witnesses to take upon themselves His name, His work of salvation, and His commandments of obedience to life-saving principles are *entitled* to have angels round about bearing them up. Consequently, a sound knowledge of the truth about angels is important.

NOTES

1. 1 Nephi 13:25–29.
2. J.R. Dummelow, ed., *A Commentary on the Holy Bible* (New York: Macmillan, 1908), p. xvi.
3. Compare Revelation 2:1 and JST, Revelation 2:1.
4. Moroni 7:37.
5. Moroni 10:4.

Ten

JOY IN THE
PRESENCE OF ANGELS

*W*hen Christ was in Jerusalem, he touched hearts with his unconditional love and taught his followers to do the same with his parables of the lost sheep, the lost coin, and the prodigal son story where the father (symbolic of Heavenly Father) rushes forth to meet his repentant son. He enlightened the spellbound crowd pressing against him, comforting them with these words, "I say unto you, there is joy in the presence of the angels of God over one sinner that repenteth."[1]

Though Saul and Alma lived in widely disparate nations, in different times, the angel elements of their stories impact humble people significantly. If people take notice of their own need to learn, their lives can be changed.

Saul, at the time an adversary of the Christian church, was on the road to Damascus for further persecution of the followers of Christ. Suddenly a light shone from heaven, and

Saul fell to the earth. He heard the Lord's voice saying to him, "Saul, Saul, why persecutest thou me?" and he was struck blind as a sign. Later, when his sight was restored, he was baptized, "and straightway he preached Christ in the synagogues, that he is the Son of God."[2] Imagine the loss to the world if the epistles and writings of this great reformed zealot of the gospel had not been reclaimed by an angel of God . . . even Jesus!

Alma's story introduces an element of making certain that children are taught the gospel so they don't grow up in disbelief. It is a constant need. Young Alma, for example, and his friends the sons of Mosiah had been children at the time of King Benjamin's last sermon, given to the King by an angel.[3] The record clearly says that because they were little children they didn't understand the king's words about the gospel. Maybe all the adults had been so busy with their meeting schedules or their family history, temple work or food storage, there wasn't time enough to teach the children effectively about the gospel truths King Benjamin had spelled out. What was the result? A generation later, we read, "It came to pass that there were many of the rising generation that could not understand the words of king Benjamin, being little children at the time he spake unto his people; and they did not believe."[4] Because of their unbelief they grew up with their hearts hardened. They would not be baptized and remained in a carnal state. They used their free agency to make choices that were unsupported by correct principles. They did not govern themselves properly. Among those who strayed were Alma, the son of the prophet Alma, and the sons of Mosiah who went about actively and wickedly campaigning against God's Church! It was embarrassing and heartbreaking to the prophet Alma, of course, and many people were led astray.[5]

Talk about destroying angels at work! These young men had fallen right into Satan's trap to deter the work of the Lord. But Alma, the grieving father, never gave up on his son. He persisted in prayer, and one day an angel of the Lord appeared to the rebellious Alma the Younger, as he is known. This angel descended from a cloud, startling the young man. He called young Alma by name. The angel spoke "in a voice of thunder" that caused the earth to shake so wildly that the young men fell to the ground. The angel then commanded Alma to stand up and explain why he persecuted the Church of God, emphasizing that they all would be totally cast out if it did not stop. Alma was so amazed that he had actually seen an angel and had actually heard a heavenly voice with his own ears that he fell back to the earth struck dumb. He couldn't even open his mouth.

After the angel departed, the sons of Mosiah carried their friend home to his father and tried to explain what had happened. The people gathered round astonished. Then began a community fasting and prayer that Alma the Younger would have his mouth opened, that he would understand the power of God unto repentance. The young men repented. They became new creatures. Surely the angels of heaven rejoiced with Alma's father and his people, and we today rejoice in being strengthened by Alma's words in the Book of Mormon.[6] The same angel who had appeared to Alma when he was up to no good returned to comfort him as he was sorrowing over the sins of the people. What a reunion! The angel said, "Blessed art thou, Alma; therefore, lift up thy head and rejoice, . . . for thou hast been faithful in keeping the commandments of God from the time which thou receivedst thy first message from him. Behold, I am he that delivered it unto you."[7]

When the infamous Jezebel was seeking the life of the prophet Elijah, he escaped into the wilderness and paused to rest beneath the shade of a juniper tree. Suddenly, an angel came and touched him and said, "Arise and eat." Elijah looked: there was a cake on the coals of a fire and a "cruse of water at his head." Elijah ate and then rested again until the angel came a second time, touched him, and told him to arise and eat because the journey was so long ahead of him. The angel warned and actually did for Elijah what he could not do for himself under the circumstances. Elijah went forth unharmed.[8]

In another period of time, certain Hebrews, including the exemplary young Daniel, were taken captive and trained in the court of Nebuchadnezzer for his purposes. The youths abstained from the meat and drink offered him from the king's own table. Though Daniel was thrust into the lions' den by the mocking king, he was protected by angels because of his obedience to God's standards. To the surprise of the doubting king, Daniel said, "My God hath sent his angel, and hath shut the lions' mouths, that they have not hurt me." Instead the men who had accused Daniel before the king were, with their families, thrown into the den of lions and destroyed.[9]

Surely many have marveled at the exciting Bible story of Shadrach, Meshach, and Abednego, who were protected from a fiery death by the appearance of angels. The illustration of this incident in my own childhood book of Bible stories is still absolutely engraved upon my heart and in my mind: the tall cone shape of the furnace; people stoking the fuel through an arched opening and cringing back from the wild, licking flames; the exotic costumes of the star players in this historical event. I remember the artist's interpretation of an angel—no wings but illuminated with a light brighter than the hot fire of the furnace.

The story line was better than any Star Wars scenario. King Nebuchadnezzar had told the three Israelite captives of war that unless they ceased worshipping their God, he would destroy them by fire. Their refusal was countered with the full pagan tradition of the court at that time. The three men were tightly bound while fully dressed so that they would catch fire more readily. The king and his barbarians stood around to watch the grizzly spectacle. Suddenly in the midst of the fire a fourth figure appeared—and no one was burning! The account reads: "Then Nebuchadnezzar the king . . . rose up in haste, and spake, and said unto his counselors, Did not we cast three men bound into the midst of the fire? They answered and said unto the king, True, O king. He answered and said, Lo, I see four men loose, walking in the midst of the fire, and they have no hurt; and the form of the fourth is like the Son of God." He called them from the fire. The startled people gathered round and realized that the fire had no power over these captives—not a hair was singed, their clothing didn't even smell of smoke. The astounded king repented. He had learned a mighty lesson about the power of the Israelite God. He repented and promoted the three Israelites to a province in Babylon where they would worship as they pleased![10]

Many prophets have had experiences with angels who have come either to save them from another's wickedness or who themselves have had personal need to repent before their predestined mission on earth could be accomplished. In the case of Nephi son of Lehi, he was accosted by his brothers Laman and Lemuel when they were trying to recover the family records from Laban. They were leaving Jerusalem before its destruction, and heaven had commanded that they retrieve the records. As they tried, Laban's servants chased them away, causing them to lose all the precious valuables they had brought along to use as bribes, if necessary. The angry brothers blamed Nephi and began beating him with a rod. Suddenly, "an angel of the Lord" stood before them commanding them to stop. He said that the Lord had chosen Nephi to be a ruler over his brethren because of their iniquities. Before the angel departed, he commanded that they go back and get the plates. The brothers repented for a time (though murmuring was their habit!), and together they did accomplish their mission. The Lord, as the angel had promised, did deliver Laban into their hands. Nephi later wrote, "I was led by the Spirit, not knowing before hand the things which I should do." Nephi secured the exquisite sword of Laban as well as the brass plates so important for their new life in the promised land. He also was given spiritual strength to convince Laban's servant to join them so that he couldn't tell of the news of their escape.

Thus they foiled those who were bent on destroying Jerusalem.[11]

The angelic appearance to bring the brothers to repentance saved Nephi. Now, ultimately, God's purposes could be done. What these young men had obtained from Laban was passed from generation to generation. At last these things finally came into custody of their descendants Mormon and then Moroni. Moroni abridged and hid the plates with other sacred items. We know that hundreds of years later this same Moroni returned to earth as an angel to give Joseph Smith custody of those plates which he then translated.

Amazing help comes to people important to God's purposes today. The woman who figures in the following incident told me her story personally and gave permission for my use of it to help other people, so long as she remained anonymous. We will call her Adelaide.

Adelaide had a spiritual experience in order to bring about a necessary repentance on her part. At the time of the incident, she was the wife of a newly called Church leader who also was an important figure in the community and financially successful. She had lived a very worldly social life in keeping with their position. When her husband received the Church call, he worried because Adelaide was not totally sincere in her efforts to conform to Church standards. He was patient and loved her deeply, though her values proved embarrassing on occasion. Repeatedly and earnestly he prayed for strength and for her repentance. He was certain that his own efforts to serve the Lord were rendered ineffective because of her compromising example.

One Sunday he was speaking from the pulpit and Adelaide was seated at the end of a pew on the right side of the aisle in the chapel. While her husband was speaking, she heard her name called. It came from the aisle into her left ear. Automatically she turned toward the sound but couldn't see anyone. The same thing happened again, and she turned to the people behind her, who were oblivious to what she was experiencing. A third time the voice called out, again addressing her by name. Annoyed, Adelaide said to herself, *What is going on here? What in the world is this all about?* Then her heart began to pound. She felt a new energy, and she heard these words, "Adelaide, support thou my servant Herbert in his important calling. Prepare your life that you may be a proper helpmeet for him in his work in the kingdom of God."

Adelaide was thunderstuck and frightened. She bowed her head in shame and humility as she felt a gentle brush across her shoulders. Amazed that heaven had noted her problem, she later told me, "An angel had touched me, and I found the courage to do what I had to do." She changed her life and found joy in supporting her husband and being obedient to God's commands.

We may not always *see* angels, but their presence can be felt or a voice heard that is lifting and helpful. That is the kind of experience Hipa Moir had when he returned to his native Samoa to fill a mission. One day Hipa and three other missionaries were driving in an open four-wheel-drive vehicle during a record-breaking typhoon. Suddenly he heard a voice command loudly: "STOP!" He stopped, then turned to his companion and asked, "Why did you tell me to stop?" His companion said, "I didn't." Hipa then asked the two elders in the back who told him to stop. They said, "We didn't." Then Hipa got out and walked to the front of the Jeep to find that the road had been washed away, leaving a deep drop a few feet in front of the vehicle. A river flowed swiftly in the new cut, all from the storm raging around them. Obviously, driving into that would have been serious. Hipa's belief is that we should *look for the miracles in our lives.*

Angels do not pop on a scene or fly through the heavens simply to please mankind. They do God's will in the serious pursuit of helping to bring about the fruits of the Atonement of Christ. They combat the forces or followers of Satan.

NOTES

1. Luke 15:10.
2. See Acts 9:1–31.
3. See Mosiah 3:1–4.
4. Mosiah 26:1.
5. See Mosiah 27:8–10.
6. See Mosiah 27:24.
7. Alma 8:15.
8. See 1 Kings 19:5–7.
9. Daniel 6:22.
10. See Daniel 3:24–25; see also verses 26–30.
11. See 1 Nephi 3:10–4:38.

Eleven

SEEING
AND BELIEVING

$\mathcal{A}$ people in ancient America built themselves a great city and named it after a city their ancestors had left years before. The population of this particular community lived in their own version of fast traffic—lavish, riotous, frivolous, sophisticated. This took place less than one hundred years before the birth of Christ. A great missionary named Aaron came among them to preach repentance. (How tireless and patient is God as each generation repeats the same mistakes!) Aaron was prepared and passionate about serving the Lord, but these people weren't interested in his prophecies. His sermon was so powerful, however, that contention arose among the listeners. One among the crowd gathered to mock cried out: "What is that thou hast testified? Hast thou seen an angel?" The debate that ensued echoes in our own day—signs for proof. Aaron was attacked. The scoffers persisted, "Why do not angels appear unto us now?" was the cry. "We do not believe that thou knowest any such thing. We do not believe in these foolish traditions."[1] Many in our day do not believe in these foolish traditions either.

Franz Werful's popular classic film *The Song of Bernadette* was based on a true incident that occurred in France in 1858. It had to do with visions and angels experienced by an innocent maiden and what she endured from irate, scoffing villagers. At the beginning of this wonderful movie, a caveat flashed on the screen: "To the believer no explanation is needed; to the disbeliever no explanation will help."

As we learn more about angels, we begin to appreciate the plan and purpose of life as well as the power of Heavenly Father. We sense his literal image and his abiding nature. We come to understand that we—like angels—were literally created like him. This more encompassing knowledge strengthens our efforts to be Christlike, to feel after him, to reach toward him, to rise up and meet him—and to believe that he sends his angels forth for the good of mortals. Mormon said, "Neither have angels ceased to minister unto the children of men."[2] And Mormon would know!

The Creator desires that mortals have a rich life experience on earth and learn those principles necessary for reentry into the heavens. Thus he has provided us with endowments, commandments, ordinances, prophets, teachers, examples, and experiences for progress and understanding—and *angels in our midst*.

The vision of Enoch is one of the most exciting to read and ponder. Enoch, as have other prophets, beheld God's creations, which included Noah and all the families of the earth, unfolding God's plan from the beginning to the Second Coming. This included a vision of some people who would "esteem not" the words of God. Then Enoch saw hosts of angels linking heaven with earth in a *crescendo of continuum*. Enoch recorded that he saw angels descending out of heaven, bearing testimony of the Father and the Son. Then the Holy Ghost fell on many and they were caught up by the powers of heaven into the peace and mercy of God.[3]

The Lord God also said to Enoch that he should advise the people that they must choose who would serve the Lord God who made them.[4] They did and they were caught up to heaven! It is clear, as there is no city of Enoch in our day— no angels thousands and thousands strong shepherding a perfect community to heaven. Perhaps we should teach and learn the basics one more time! And as we are converted we can strengthen others. Elder Jeffrey Holland spoke to delegates of a Church Educational System conference and said, "I believe that we need to speak of and believe in and bear testimony to the ministry of angels more. . . . They constitute one of God's great methods of witnessing through the veil.[5]

When the grave of my older brother was dedicated recently, his son Scott prayed with unusual insight to Heavenly Father that this fine man would be given "the privilege of serving as a guardian angel for the grandchildren left behind on earth." The plea was that these growing children might be thus protected and enhanced. This was a deeply moving and spiritual experience for those of us gathered around that quiet plot of ground that would hold this grandfather's earthly body.

In a sermon at the funeral of my husband's grandmother Elizabeth Hoagland Cannon, wife of President George Q. Cannon, President Joseph F. Smith pronounced some enlightening and comforting information regarding angels. He said that the angels who minister to this earth are not strangers, "but from the ranks of our kindred, friends, and fellow-beings and fellow-servants. . . . Our fathers and mothers, brothers, sisters and friends who have passed away from this earth, having been faithful, and worthy to enjoy these rights and privileges, may have a mission given to them to visit their relatives and friends upon the earth again, bringing from the divine Presence messages of love, of warning, or reproof and instruction, to those whom they had learned to love in the flesh. And so it is with Sister Cannon. She can return and visit her friends, provided it be in accordance with the wisdom of the Almighty."[6]

A friend of mine had been born a twin, but her twin died early. Then she lost another brother, and later her mother died. Then her first daughter drowned while just a toddler. For many years she had faithfully controlled her grief. Then this season her beloved father died. In addition she became very ill and overworked from serving others with her unique skill in physical therapy and nutrition. Dolly had received a blessing from her husband and then rested in her bed, silently praying and drawing close to the Lord. Suddenly she began to feel a surge of energy about her. It was marvelous. There appeared before her these lost family members whom she had so dearly loved and missed. She is careful not to speak of this unless moved upon by the Holy Ghost. But she can bear strong witness of eternal life and of God's goodness.

In our own hours of deepest heartbreak or enlivening personal testimony, God can use us in our humble way to testify that what he says is true: "I Jesus have sent mine angel to testify unto you these things. . . . Come. And let him that heareth say, Come. And let him that is athirst come. And whosoever will, let him take the water of life freely."[7]

There is evidence to support the idea that those who have sacred spiritual experiences have an obligation, a duty, to set forth the truth. I firmly believe that we are to help stem the tide of error. When we are converted to a principle, we are counseled to share with others and strengthen them. Whether they accept or not is their choice. Joseph Smith said, "There are many yet on the earth among all sects, parties, and denominations, who are blinded by the subtle craftiness of men, whereby they lie in wait to deceive, and who are only kept from the truth because they know not where to find it."[8] Even a small voice can make a difference in the opinions or beliefs of others. The phenomenal growth of the Church is indicative of the need for that. As the Prophet Joseph continued, "A very large ship is benefited very much by a very small helm in the time of a storm."[9]

Joseph gave that counsel to guide the Saints persecuted by their neighbors, but it also applies to those who have received a witness of truth regarding angels so that misconceptions regarding this manifestation of God's love for his mortal children may be rectified. Several years after Joseph Smith was martyred, he returned to earth as an angel—a spiritual being—and appeared to President Brigham Young. Among other things, Joseph told Brigham Young: "Tell the brethren to be humble and faithful and be sure to keep the Spirit of the Lord, that it will lead them aright. Be careful and not turn away the still, small voice; it will teach them what to do and where to go; it will yield the fruits of the kingdom. Tell the brethren to keep their hearts open to conviction, so that when the Holy Ghost comes to them, their hearts will be ready to receive."[10]

Faith comes and signs follow the believer.[11] God said *angels* were his. The burden of proof is ours. *Hast thou seen an angel?*

NOTES

1. Alma 21:5, 8.

2. Moroni 7:29.

3. See Moses 6, 7.

4. See Moses 7:10–21.

5. Jeffrey R. Holland, Book of Mormon Symposium, Brigham Young University, Provo, Utah; 9 August 1994.

6. Joseph F. Smith, *Gospel Doctrine* (Salt Lake City: Deseret Book Co., 1939), pp. 435, 436.

7. Revelation 22:16–17.

8. Doctrine and Covenants 123:12.

9. Doctrine and Covenants 123:16.

10. As cited by Marion G. Romney, in Conference Report, April 1944, p. 141.

11. See Mark 16:17.

EPILOGUE

*W*e honor God's prophets, who are ordained and sustained to reveal truth to Heavenly Father's children. Their validation of the nature of angels is important to a sincere person's faith. The Lord Jesus Christ said, "By mine own voice out of the heavens, . . . I have given the heavenly hosts of mine angels charge concerning you."[1] Jacob said, "For I truly had seen angels, and they had ministered to me."[2] A similar statement has been recorded for prophets in every dispensation of time. The following thoughts confirm the immortality of the soul and the hope that God still sends angels to help mortals through this life. It remains for people to learn to recognize them.

Old Testament: "The Lord God of heaven, . . . he shall send his angel before thee."[3]

119

New Testament: "I say unto you, there is joy in the presence of the angels of God."[4]

Book of Mormon: "Neither have angels ceased to minister unto the children of men."[5]

Doctrine and Covenants: "Mine angels round about you, to bear you up."[6]

Joseph Smith: "If you live up to your privileges, the angels cannot be restrained from being your associates."[7]

Brigham Young: "Our spirits once dwelt in the heavens and were as pure and holy as angels."[8]

John Taylor: "The angels are our watchmen. . . . The angels gather the elect, and pluck out all that offends."[9]

Lorenzo Snow: "Now if you want to get heaven within you, and to get into heaven, you want to pursue that course that angels do who are in heaven. If you want to know how you are to increase, I will tell you, it is by getting godliness within you."[10]

Wilford Woodruff: "There will be no disappointment as to the blessings promised those who sincerely worship Him. . . . The sweet whisperings of the Holy Spirit will be given to them and the treasures of Heaven, the communion of angels, will be added from time to time, for His promise has gone forth and it cannot fail!"[11]

Joseph F. Smith: "The man who passes through this probation, and is faithful, being redeemed from sin by the blood of Christ, through the ordinances of the gospel, and attains to exaltation in the kingdom of God, is not less but greater than the angels, and if you doubt it, read your Bible, for there it is written that the Saints shall 'judge angels.' "[12]

Heber J. Grant: "The Savior appeared to Joseph Smith and to Oliver Cowdery, and that Moses, and Elias and Elijah also appeared and conferred upon them all the keys of all the dispensations of the gospel that have ever existed upon the earth."[13]

George Albert Smith: "The Lord said that the destroying angels should pass by us and not slay us if we kept his counsel."[14]

David O. McKay: "Death cannot touch the spirit. . . . If there is any truth that is taught through the gospel of Jesus Christ, it is the truth of the immortality of the soul."[15]

Joseph Fielding Smith: "The physical death . . . is not a permanent separation of the spirit and the tabernacle of flesh, notwithstanding the fact that the body returns again to the elements. It is only a temporary separation which shall cease at the resurrection day, when the body shall be called forth from the dust, animated by spirit, to live again."[16]

Harold B. Lee: "Wouldn't you like to so live that when God spoke you would be able to hear it, or to be able to be worthy to have a visitation from an angelic visitor, or perhaps to be ready to go into the presence of the Lord? The Lord told us how we could be ready."[17]

Spencer W. Kimball: "Get a notebook, my young folks, a journal that will last through all time, and maybe the angels may quote from it for eternity."[18]

Ezra Taft Benson: "I promise you, dear children, that angels will minister unto you also. You may not see them, but they will be there to help you, and you will feel of their presence."[19]

Howard W. Hunter: "Even with the logic of nature's regeneration and even with the testimony of that empty garden tomb, there are still those who feel the grave is a final destination. But the doctrine of the Resurrection is the single most fundamental and crucial doctrine in the Christian religion. It cannot be overemphasized, nor can it be disregarded."[20]

Gordon B. Hinckley: "How marvelous a gift, that if we live worthy we shall have the right to the company of angels. Here is protection, here is guidance, here is direction—all of these from powers beyond our own natural gifts."[21]

*   *   *

We are blessed to be witnesses that not only are there prophets of God among us but also angels of God. The very thought of such things is like losing oneself in a sky of endless stars. The Spirit within us softens and swells, the heart warms, a sweep of well-being lifts. Gratitude to God overflows for his hosts of angels, his vast family of mortals and immortals, his infinitely varied creations, his plan of happiness that brings beautiful experiences and assuages the wrenching ones.

NOTES

1. Doctrine and Covenants 84:42.
2. Jacob 7:15.
3. Genesis 24:7.
4. Luke 15:10.
5. Moroni 7:29.
6. Doctrine and Covenants 84:88.
7. Joseph Smith, *Teachings of the Prophet Joseph Smith*, comp. Joseph Fielding Smith (Salt Lake City: Deseret Book Co., 1976), p. 226.
8. Brigham Young, *Discourses of Brigham Young*, comp. John A. Widtsoe (Salt Lake City: Deseret Book Co., 1976), p. 51.
9. John Taylor, *The Gospel Kingdom*, comp. G. Homer Durham (Salt Lake City: Bookcraft, 1964), p. 31.
10. Lorenzo Snow, *The Teachings of Lorenzo Snow*, ed. Clyde J. Williams (Salt Lake City: Bookcraft, 1984), p. 148.
11. In James R. Clark, ed., *Messages of the First Presidency*, 3:244.
12. Joseph F. Smith, *Gospel Doctrine* (Salt Lake City: Deseret Book Co., 1976), p. 18.
13. Heber J. Grant, in Conference Report, April 1928, p. 9.
14. George Albert Smith, in Conference Report, October 1945, p. 21.
15. David O. McKay, *Gospel Ideals* (Salt Lake City: The Improvement Era, 1953), p. 56.
16. Joseph Fielding Smith, *Doctrines of Salvation*, comp. Bruce R. McConkie, 3 vols. (Salt Lake City: Bookcraft, 1954–56), 2:216–17.

17. Harold B. Lee, *The Teachings of Harold B. Lee,* ed. Clyde J. Williams (Salt Lake City: Bookcraft, 1996), p. 429.

18. Spencer W. Kimball, *The Teachings of Spencer W. Kimball,* ed. Edward L. Kimball (Salt Lake City: Bookcraft, 1982), p. 351.

19. Ezra Taft Benson, in Conference Report, April 1989, p. 105.

20. Howard W. Hunter, in Conference Report, April 1986, p. 18.

21. Gordon B. Hinckley, in Vacaville–Santa Rosa Regional Conference, 21 May 1995.

INDEX

125

INDEX

names of, 53–55
physical characteristics of, 48–50,
 52, 54–55, 93–94, 112
protection of, 51, 104–6
purpose of, 11, 56, 67–68, 106
residing in heaven and earth, 66
testimonies of, 96–97, 111
use of priesthood authority, 33–34,
 49, 51
visitations of, 6–27, 52, 77
as witnesses, 27, 60
See also Destroying angels;
 Guardian angels; Heavenly
 hosts; Spiritual beings
Anger, 17
Apostasy, 94–95, 98
Atonement, 109, 120

— B —

Baptism, 2–3, 59–60, 98
Benjamin (King), 56, 82
 on believing in God, 41
Benson, Ezra Taft, on feeling the pres-
 ence of angels, 121
Bible, validity of, 94–95, 97, 120
Bible Commentary (book), 96
Blessings, priesthood, 33–34
 temporal, 59, 78
Book of Mormon, 49, 58, 83–84,
 106–7, 120
Brown, Hugh B., reports seeing
 Harold B. Lee, 91
Buehner, Paul, 88–89

— C —

Callings, of angels, 32, 37, 69
 blessings associated with, 36
 heavenly help with, 7, 22–26

Casilles, Henri, on importance of
 names, 54
Celestial glory, 60, 78
Children, teaching gospel to, 102
Christmas, 73
Comfort, 25, 32, 51
Conversion, 113
Countenance, 11, 15, 57
Covenants, 68, 95, 100
Cowley, Matthew, role in dedication of
 Los Angeles Temple, 89–90
Creation, spiritual, 41–42
Crucifixion, 82
Crusades, 96

— D —

Dallin, Cyrus E. (sculptor), 86–87
Daniel, 104
Death, 6–7, 60, 114, 121
 comfort after, 12–13, 15–16, 31
 life after, 11–12
Destroying angels, 121
Determination, 24
Discouragement, 16, 26–27
Divorce, 22
Doctrine and Covenants, on angels
 round about, 120
Dummelow, *Bible Commentary*, 96

— E —

Elias, 76, 121
Elijah, 104, 121
Enoch, 112–13
Example, 20, 107

— F —

Fairbanks, Avard Tennyson (sculptor), 87

126

INDEX

Faith, gaining knowledge through, 34,
    99–100
  loss of, 97
  in love of God, 13, 36
  visitation of angels based on, 49,
    57, 60, 66, 68
Faithfulness, 10, 11, 27, 116
Family, as angels, 11–12, 19–20,
    20–21, 51, 114–15
  heavenly, 3, 95
  importance of, 22, 61–62
Fasting, 103
Fear, 14, 16, 21, 72
Forgiveness, 18, 49

— G —

Gabriel, angel, 54, 75
  message to Zacharias, 57
Genealogy, angelic help with, 33
Gifts, spiritual, 43
God, 27, 37
  belief in, 13, 36, 58–59
  and biblical translations, 97
  creator, 41, 59
  laws of, 43, 60
  love of, 11
  mindfulness of, toward servants, 8,
    23–26, 34, 36, 65, 104–6
  names of, 41–42
  relationship with man, 66–67
  temporal gifts of, 17, 59, 78
  work of, 11, 43, 79
  worship of, 25, 49, 73, 105
  See also Jesus Christ; Heavenly Fa-
    ther
Gold plates. *See* Book of Mormon
Gospel, 56, 95, 97
  See also Restoration
Grant, Heber J., on restoration of

priesthood keys, 121
  dedication of Hill Cumorah monu-
    ment, 84
Gratitude, 11, 22
Great and abominable church, 94–95
Guardian angels, 5, 35–36, 37, 75, 113

— H —

Hamlet, 65
Hanks, Marion D., on familial relation-
    ships of angels, 68
Happiness, 12, 26, 41, 89
Heaven, 7, 58–59, 120
Heavenly Father, 3, 82, 112
  family of, 3, 42
  sending angels as answers to prayer,
    9
  See also God
Heavenly hosts, 5, 72, 78, 113, 119
Hinckley, Gordon B., on keys of Aa-
    ronic priesthood, 36–37
  on right to company of angels, 122
  on truth about angels, 37
Holland, Jeffrey, on speaking of angels,
    113
Holy Ghost, 56, 61, 66
  as a guide, 37–38, 106, 116
  moves one to speak, 38, 66–67,
    114–15
  outpouring of Spirit, 10, 19, 26,
    35, 113, 120
  role in birth of Christ, 75
  witness of truth, 5, 84, 100
Holy Day of Pentecost, 52
Hope, 17, 21
House of Israel, 44
Humility, 49, 108, 116
Hunter, Howard W., on the resurrec-
    tion, 122

127